The Miracles of Jesus

Finding God in Desperate Moments

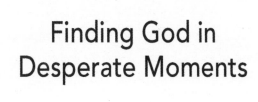

Jessica LaGrone

Abingdon Women / Nashville

The Miracles of Jesus
Finding God in Desperate Moments

Copyright © 2017 Abingdon Press

This book is printed on elemental chlorine-free paper.

ISBN 978-1-5018-3545-2

19 20 21 22 23 24 25 26 — 10 9 8 7 6 5 4

MANUFACTURED IN THE UNITED STATES OF AMERICA

CONTENTS

About the Author

Jessica LaGrone is Dean of the Chapel at Asbury Theological Seminary in Wilmore, Kentucky, and an acclaimed pastor, teacher, and speaker whose engaging communication style endears her to groups and audiences throughout the United States. A native of Texas, Jessica previously served as Pastor of Creative Ministries at The Woodlands United Methodist Church near Houston, Texas. She is the author of numerous studies including *The Rewritten Life: When God Changes Your Story*, *Set Apart: Holy Habits of Prophets and Kings*, *Broken and Blessed: How God Changed the World Through One Imperfect Family*, and *Namesake: When God Rewrites Your Story*. She also is the author of one book, also titled *Broken and Blessed*, a contributor to the all-church Advent study *Under Wraps*, and a video host for *Disciple Fast Track*. Jessica and her husband, Jim, have two young children, Drew and Kate.

Follow Jessica:

Twitter: @JessicaLaGrone

Instagram: @jixsalagrone

Facebook: @jessicalagrone

Blog: JessicaLaGrone.com
                   (check here for event dates and booking information)

Introduction

Jesus demonstrated the presence and power of God by performing miracles. He turned water into wine, healed the sick, calmed the storm, opened blind eyes, and raised the dead. While these beloved stories draw our attention to divine power, they also have something else in common: human desperation. Every time we see Jesus performing a miracle, we also get a glimpse into the gift of desperation, a gift that opens us to the dramatic power of God through our desperate need for Him.

In this six-week study, we will explore many of the miracles of Jesus, helping us see that our weakness is an invitation for God to work powerfully in our lives and reminding us that we need God on our best days just as much as we do on our worst.

Themes and miracle stories include

- the gift of desperation (turning water into wine and other signs of God)
- the miracle of abundance (feeding the five thousand and other abundance stories)
- miracles on the water (calming the storm, walking on water, the abundant catch)
- Jesus our healer who restores (five stories of healing)
- the power of God's compassion and love (Jairus's daughter and the bleeding woman)
- the miracle we all receive (the Incarnation)

Getting Started

For each week of our study, there are five readings. Each of these readings includes the following segments:

Read God's Word	All or part of the miracle story (and/or other key Scriptures)
Reflect and Respond	A guided reflection and study of the biblical story with space for recording your responses (blue-gray type indicates write-in-the-book questions or activities)
Talk with God	A sample prayer to guide you into a personal time of prayer

You will be able to complete each reading in about twenty to thirty minutes. Completing these readings each week will help prepare you for the discussion and activities of the group session.

Once a week you will gather with your group to watch a video in which I share additional insights into the miracle stories and their application in our lives. I encourage you to discuss what you're learning and to share how God is working in your own life to demonstrate His miraculous power and love. Sharing with one another will enable you to recognize God's power and activity in your lives more clearly and help you encourage and pray for one another.

Before you begin this journey, give God permission to work in your heart and life. Offer yourself to Him and express your desperate desire to know Him more intimately and see His power at work in your life—on your best days as well as your worst days. He is a God who still works miracles!

Jessica

Week 1

THE GIFT OF DESPERATION

What Happens When We Run Out

DAY 1: THE QUESTION OF MIRACLES

Read God's Word

¹In the beginning was the Word, and the Word was with God, and the Word was God. ²He was in the beginning with God. ³All things came into being through him, and without him not one thing came into being. What has come into being ⁴in him was life, and the life was the light of all people. ⁵The light shines in the darkness, and the darkness did not overcome it.

⁶There was a man sent from God, whose name was John. ⁷He came as a witness to testify to the light, so that all might believe through him. ⁸He himself was not the light, but he came to testify to the light. ⁹The true light, which enlightens everyone, was coming into the world.

¹⁰He was in the world, and the world came into being through him; yet the world did not know him. ¹¹He came to what was his own, and his own people did not accept him. ¹²But to all who received him, who believed in his name, he gave power to become children of God, ¹³who were born, not of blood or of the will of the flesh or of the will of man, but of God.

¹⁴And the Word became flesh and lived among us, and we have seen his glory, the glory as of a father's only son, full of grace and truth.

(John 1:1-14)

Reflect and Respond

Miracles started out for me as a problem to be solved.

I'm a scientist by training. I spent much of my undergraduate years in a science lab: experimenting, observing, and writing up hypotheses about the evidence found. About halfway through college I experienced a radical change of direction that took me from medicine to ministry. God got my attention in some pretty significant ways—some of which I would even call miraculous—communicating that I'd be serving Him in ministry, not medicine. But even though my calling changed, the way my brain works did not.

Here's what I mean: I'm still pretty analytical by nature, and sometimes I find myself applying the scientific method to the work of ministry. I've even caught myself approaching pastoral counseling as if experimenting in a lab! (There's nothing more comforting than pouring your heart out to your pastor about your problems and hearing this response, "Well, let's lay out the possible variables in this system and hypothesize the quantitative change they might enact on the observed outcomes.")

OK, so I don't actually say it out loud, but I do sometimes have a hard time remembering that human nature is not a scientific or measurable quantity. I've discovered that God made me just the way I am—analytical and science-minded—and God has plans to use every bit of who I am to serve Him. I had an idea of who I was and what I would do with my life; who I am didn't change, but God had in mind something very different for me to do. Even when God changes the direction of our lives, He still uses the way we're wired to serve Him.

When I read the miracle stories in the Bible, I sometimes find myself putting my scientist's hat on. Scientists ask questions and look for answers, and I have a lot of questions.

I wish I were standing next to Moses as the Red Sea parted, holding a tensiometer to measure the surface tension of the water as it pulled away from gravity. I want to be with Jesus at Cana with my test tube to find out just how H_2O (water) could possibly become CH_3CH_2OH (ethyl alcohol). I want to put monitors on Lazarus to see his vital signs as the "beep beep" of a heartbeat appears where once there was none.

I'm in good company. We see many people in the Bible asking questions about God's miraculous acts and promises to do amazing, seemingly impossible things.

Read the following Scriptures, and note the person and the question that he or she asks:

	Person(s)	Question(s)
Exodus 3:11, 13	moses	who am I
Luke 1:13-18	Zechariah	How can I be sure
Luke 1:34	Mary	How can I be expecting

Moses, Zechariah, and Mary had questions too. When it comes to the miraculous, we tend to ask two common questions.

Two Common Questions

1. *How?* My own desire to measure miracles is really birthed out of a desire to answer the many questions they raise. Most of my questions about the miracles are "how" questions. How are these things possible? How do miracles occur? How did God do that?

When you think about miracles in the Bible, what are some of the *how* questions that come to your mind?

2. *Why?* The deeply emotional side of me (it's in there battling it out with the analytical side) also has questions about miracles. Mostly they begin with the word *why?* God, why was this person miraculously healed while a child died? Why did you bring some people back from the dead while others such as your earthly father, Joseph, or your cousin John the Baptist died during your lifetime? Why do you answer some prayers for miracles and not others? If you are like me, at one time or another you have found yourself staring out into the sky as you cry out to God, "Why?"

What are some of your own *why* questions regarding miracles?

We all have *how* and *why* questions. They are part of our human experience and curiosity, and in truth, they are sometimes what drives us to God for answers. But when I read the Bible, it seems that the *how* and *why* questions aren't the first ones to be answered. Most often, we see miracles answering the question of *who*.

A Third Question: Who

I believe it's the *who* question that puts the *how* into perspective and gives us a relationship with the One who walks with us through our *why* moments in life.

What are the *who* questions that we're talking about?

Read the following Scriptures, and summarize the who question(s) you find in each:

Mark 4:41

Matthew 16:15

Job 38:25-28; 37-38

Psalm 113:5-6

The disciples' question "Who is this...?" is the beginning point of the *who* question. Who is this that can still the wind and the waves, turn water into wine, heal a blind man, raise the dead? But as we read story after story of God's great acts on earth, we begin to ask the psalmist's question "Who is like the LORD our God?" And the answer is clear: No *one*. No one is like this. No one that I've ever met before. I've never seen anyone walk on water. I've never encountered anyone who could make a river turn to blood. I've never met anyone who speaks through whirlwinds, burnings bushes, and descending doves. I've never seen anyone heal blindness with a touch.

The miracle stories describe a God who is like no one else. They often leave us in awe and wonder.

How have the miracle stories in the Bible evoked your sense of awe and wonder in God? What have they revealed to you about God?

> **The miracle stories describe a God who is like no one else. They often leave us in awe and wonder.**

The miracle stories reveal many things about God, but first and foremost they remind us that God is *transcendent*. God transcends (surpasses, goes beyond, rises above) all that we see and understand. There is nothing in our finite, earthly experience that prepares us to understand what kind of being God is and what He is capable of. When God speaks in miracles, it tells us that He is beyond everything we understand about our world and our capabilities in it.

A transcendent God, by definition, is hard to see, to touch, to understand, and most significantly, to know. But what if you were a transcendent, all-powerful God who *wanted* people to know you? What if you were a Creator trying to have a deep and personal relationship with those in your creation? How would you go about it? Would you boom with a thundering voice so that they heard your power loud and clear? Would you shake the foundations of the ground they stood on so that they sensed your presence?

Most things that you might try would probably be so frightening that no one would stick around long enough to find out what you were trying to say! It's no accident that so many encounters with God and His messengers in Scripture begin with the phrase, "Do not be afraid." To encounter God's power is a frightening experience!

I remember a story a youth minister told me when I was a teenager that helped me make sense of how God answers the *who* question for us. If you were standing above an anthill, watching the ants scurry to and fro about their work, and you were overcome with a deep love for those ants and wanted to tell them that you loved them, how would you go about telling them? I initially got stuck on this part of the story because, growing up in Texas, I had been stung by my fair share of fire ants and couldn't imagine why anyone would love ants!

You could stand over them and shout "I love you!" at the top of your lungs, but they wouldn't understand you. You could write a tiny letter and deliver it with tweezers to the center of the colony, but they couldn't read it. But if you happened to have supernatural powers, the one way you could communicate your love for the ant colony would be to become an ant yourself—to take on an ant body, learn to speak ant language, and walk into the colony looking and speaking exactly as they did in order to connect with them and tell them of your love.

The ability to translate yourself into the physical world in such a tangible, relatable, understandable way is called *immanence*, and it is the opposite of transcendence. This is the way of Jesus: to take the incomprehensible, invisible nature of God and package it in a way we can touch, feel, hear, and see.

Read John 1:14 in the margin. How do we see both transcendence and immanence in this verse?

The Word became flesh and made his dwelling among us. We have seen his glory, the glory of the one and only Son, who came from the Father, full of grace and truth. (John 1:14 NIV)

By taking on human flesh, Jesus gives us a God we can comprehend (immanence). But within that flesh "we have seen his glory" (transcendence). The transcendent power of God is acting through this first-century Jewish man.

Transcendence without immanence produces fear: God is terrifying, unrelatable, unknowable. And immanence without transcendence produces casual over-familiarity and contempt: Jesus is my buddy, just like me, and nothing in particular about my life has to change because He is part of it. But in Jesus we have the perfect balance. Fully God. Fully man. This is the Incarnation: the fullness of God putting on the fullness of human nature; the supernatural and the natural meeting in one incredible person.

If this seems a little mind-boggling for you, you're not alone! The Incarnation causes just as many problems and questions for us as it has answers.

People look at the stories of Jesus, and He looks so normal, so human. How could someone so seemingly natural do these supernatural things? This means that more people are skeptical of Jesus' miracles than many other parts of the Bible. They're often searching for the hidden trick in the miracle, the secret hoax or conspiracy embedded in these stories. This happens to me, too, when the *how* questions get a little out of control and begin to take priority.

Immanent –
being within the limits
of possible experience
or knowledge[1]

Transcendent –
exceeding usual limits;
being beyond the
limits of all possible
experience and
knowledge[2]

Although God knows that the pain of the *why* is often deeply personal and important, His deepest longing is for us to ask the *who* question that will lead us . . . into the only relationship that can make sense of the *whys* we face.

Have you ever struggled with skepticism or doubt regarding Jesus' miracles? Why or why not?

Instead, the question to ask first when you meet a miracle is the question of *who*. After all, God didn't come to earth in person to give us the *how* secrets behind His power. And although God knows that the pain of the *why* is often deeply personal and important, His deepest longing is for us to ask the *who* question that will lead us like paving stones straight into the only relationship that can make sense of the *whys* we face.

Who is the question that will take us onto the boat with the disciples, gasping at the moment a raging storm stops cold. It's the question that transports us to a tomb, staring into the tear-streaked face of a grieving friend who speaks the commanding words: "Lazarus, come out!" It will lead us to look into the eyes of compassion that see the soul of a hurting person where others see a dirty leper, a woman outcast, a blind beggar.

Asking the question "Who is this?" about the God behind the miracles will not only lead to answers; it will lead you to a person. Every single miracle will teach us something about the transcendent God and lead us closer to Him. After all, the One who walked on water, healed the lame, made the blind see, and raised people from the dead is alive and present with you as you read these stories, and He longs to be in relationship with you.

What does He want to tell you about Himself? That's the question of miracles. And that is the question we will be exploring in the days and weeks to come.

Talk with God

Gracious God, You are all at once too transcendent to understand and too immanent to ignore. Open my ears to hear the message in Your miracles. Let my questions lead me straight into Your arms. Help me to learn from Your Word and from those who are making this journey with me. May I come to know You more deeply and become more like You in all I do. Amen.

DAY 2: THE FIRST SIGN

Read God's Word

[1] *On the third day there was a wedding in Cana of Galilee, and the mother of Jesus was there.* [2] *Jesus and his disciples had also been invited to the wedding.* [3] *When the wine gave out, the mother of Jesus said to him, "They have no wine."* [4] *And Jesus said*

to her, "Woman, what concern is that to you and to me? My hour has not yet come." [5]His mother said to the servants, "Do whatever he tells you." [6]Now standing there were six stone water jars for the Jewish rites of purification, each holding twenty or thirty gallons. [7]Jesus said to them, "Fill the jars with water." And they filled them up to the brim. [8]He said to them, "Now draw some out, and take it to the chief steward." So they took it. [9]When the steward tasted the water that had become wine, and did not know where it came from (though the servants who had drawn the water knew), the steward called the bridegroom [10]and said to him, "Everyone serves the good wine first, and then the inferior wine after the guests have become drunk. But you have kept the good wine until now." [11]Jesus did this, the first of his signs, in Cana of Galilee, and revealed his glory; and his disciples believed in him.

[12]After this he went down to Capernaum with his mother, his brothers, and his disciples; and they remained there a few days.

(John 2:1-12)

Reflect and Respond

Last year my little girl got to go to her first wedding. In the past we'd found babysitters to watch her during family weddings, but Kate had turned four ("and a half," she would want me to remind you) and was getting really good at sitting quietly through church services, so we decided she was ready. I spent some time beforehand talking to her about everything that she would see, telling her about the beautiful dresses and flowers, explaining some of the wedding rituals such as rings and vows, and making sure she knew the wedding itself was a worship service meant to point us to the God who created us and wants to be united with us. She sat spellbound during the wedding, and finally, at the reception, we came to the moment she had been waiting for all day: the cake! It was a wonderful introduction to what is sure to be something she will enjoy for a lifetime.

The following week I was walking by our living room when I noticed Kate wrapping her white blanket around the horn of her favorite stuffed unicorn. When I stopped to ask what she was playing, she explained today was the big day: the unicorn was getting married too! I sat as a guest and watched her reenact many of the moments from the wedding of the previous week. It was amazing to see all she had absorbed as she began her experience of weddings and the joy found there.

Weddings are full of signs. Small, visible elements that point to a bigger reality that something incredibly important is going on. Two people walk down an aisle to meet each other, flanked by their closest friends and family. Rings, signifying an unbroken circle of love, are exchanged. Sometimes family members light two smaller candles that the couple uses to light a single candle together.

Meaningful songs are sung, prayers are prayed, and vows are exchanged as promises of what is to come.

Most of all, these signs point to a new beginning. Two people walk into a room separately, but they leave together as one. This is the first day of a new life, a new start. After today, everything will be different.

Jesus began His ministry of miracles at a wedding. The Gospel of John tells us that the changing of water into wine at a wedding near his hometown of Nazareth was the first of the signs Jesus performed. This was a new beginning for Jesus, and after this first sign nothing would be the same.

Reread John 2:11 and write it below:

Notice that John uses the word *sign* and not *miracle*. John is the only Gospel that never uses the word *miracle*. He always refers to Jesus' miraculous works as *signs*.

What are some of the physical signs in your daily life that guide you from place to place? What does each point you to?

Sign   **What It Points To**

You might have listed things such as the sign that signifies the street you're supposed to turn on to get home, or the sign that points you toward the restrooms in a crowded shopping mall. If you are excited to see these signs, it's not because of the sign itself but because of what it points to.

Signs exist to call our attention to something more important, to act as the guide to what we are looking for. John tells miracle stories to point us to Jesus. Jesus uses signs during this wedding miracle to drop hints about what His own ministry will be about. Since this is the first miracle, He packs it full of signs that point to His purpose and character.

Let's explore three of the signs that show up at the wedding at Cana.

1. Water

~ *Water is a sign of new creation.* In the very beginning of Genesis, "the Spirit of God was hovering over the waters" (1:2 NIV). Creation begins with water, and

Jesus uses signs during this wedding miracle to drop hints about what His own ministry will be about.

John is the Gospel that takes us back to the beginning. John's Gospel doesn't start with Jesus' birth but goes all the way back to echo the Creation story: "In the beginning was the Word, and the Word was with God, and the Word was God" (John 1:1). In the ministry of Jesus, God is starting all over again to restore the world to the newness of Eden.

Water is a sign of cleansing and purification. Water is what we call the universal solvent because it's able to dissolve more substances than any other liquid. When we go to wash our hands, our dishes, or our cars, we use water because it has the ability to surround and break down almost any impurity.

When Jesus asked the servants at the wedding to bring Him some water, He did so in an incredibly specific way.

Reread John 2:6-7. What did Jesus ask the servants to bring Him?

How big were these jars?

What was their purpose?

In Jewish practices, coming near to God meant getting clean first. There were laws about impurity and how to get cleansed. Ritual washing was a way of seeking closeness to their Creator, and these jars were the containers meant for that purpose. Those at the party couldn't look at these jars without thinking about a ritual of physical washing that equaled spiritual purity.

Through Jesus' ministry, God turned the tables by being the One to bring spiritual cleansing to His people instead of waiting for them to clean themselves up before they could come close to Him.

2. Wine

Wine is a sign of joy. The Jews had a saying: "Without wine, there is no joy."[3] Wine was a symbol of joy, and Jesus was bringing joy in overflowing abundance. A wedding party really needed over a hundred gallons of wine, especially one that had already run through their preplanned portion. So this sign of overflowing joy reminds us of Jesus' desire to give us more than just "enough" for our lives.

37"Do not judge, and you will not be judged; do not condemn, and you will not be condemned. Forgive, and you will be forgiven; 38give, and it will be given to you. A good measure, pressed down, shaken together, running over, will be put into your lap; for the measure you give will be the measure you get back."

(Luke 6:37-38)

Compared with the ministry of Moses, who turned water into blood as a sign of God's judgment (Exodus 7:14-24), Jesus will change this ordinary substance of water into wine as a sign of joy.

This may be a good time to mention that the association of wine and joy was not about drunkenness. Intoxication was considered a disgrace, and any mention of drunkenness in Scripture is associated with sin. In Jesus' day wine was the primary beverage for adults—safe to drink and somewhat more diluted than what we are used to today. So, the mention of wine in abundance would not have meant drunkenness but joy. Joy is a response to abundance.

Read Luke 6:37-38 in the margin. How does Jesus encourage us to use abundance in practicing forgiveness and kindness to others?

Write down any words used in these verses associated with wine and the abundance of God's love. (You might want to look at more than one version.)

How do these verses suggest an ongoing cycle of abundance?

Wine is a sensory sign. Psalm 34:8 encourages us to "taste and see that the Lord is good." Scripture uses sensory language about God's goodness to help us remember that God is as real and tangible as the things we can taste, touch, and see with our senses. "May God be as real to you as the things right in front of your face," it is saying. In other words, may God's goodness explode before your eyes with the joy of the face of your loved one, or in your mouth as the hot chocolate that hits your tongue. May you not only know about the love of God but also experience it deeply.

Wine is also a sign of the Messiah. An abundance of wine is often used in the Old Testament to symbolize the blessings in the promised kingdom of God and the arrival of the Messiah.

Read Joel 3:17-18. What are some of the blessings in the promised Kingdom named in these verses?

Thirst and dryness indicate that God's people are longing for the Messiah to come, while overflowing, dripping new wine is a signpost that the Messiah has come. In Isaiah 24, we find a dry and painful description of God's people and their situation. And then in chapter 25, we read of a banquet, held on a mountain, in celebration of the arrival of the Messiah. The wine and rich foods of the celebration are a sign that points to other joys the Messiah will bring.

Read Isaiah 25:6-9. What are some of these joys the Messiah will bring?

We not only have these joys of the coming Kingdom to look forward to but we also have the joys of Christ in this life. What are some of the joys that He has brought into your life?

3. Weddings

The last sign is that of the wedding itself. Then, as now, weddings were occasions of great joy. Along with the Passover celebration, a wedding was the greatest day of celebration a community could experience.

Instead of being about only two people, a wedding is a gathering of an entire community to focus on love, hope, and unity. Weddings are not meant to be an exclusionary love of two people witnessed by bystanders. They are meant to point everyone present to the love of God.

Jesus chose the occasion of a wedding to show the power of God working through Him for the first time. Throughout the Scriptures we see a connection between weddings and God's kingdom.

Throughout the Scriptures we see a connection between weddings and God's kingdom.

Read the following Scriptures, and note how each uses a wedding as a symbol or sign of the Kingdom:

Isaiah 62:1-5

Matthew 22:1-14

The angel said to me, "Write this: Blessed are those who are invited to the marriage supper of the Lamb." And he said to me, "These are true words of God."

(Revelation 19:9)

There are signs of God's love all around us every day, pointing us to Jesus.

Now read Revelation 19:9 in the margin. How does God use the picture of a wedding feast here? What does it indicate?

Talk about abundant joy! One day we will finally and joyfully be fully united with God forever!

Remember what I said about weddings? All the signs in a wedding point to a new beginning. Two people walk into a room separately, but they leave together. This is the first day of a new life, a new start. After today, everything will be different.

Jesus is starting off His ministry with a wedding to say, "This is the beginning of something you have never seen before, and nothing will ever be the same again. I want to bring joy, purity, new creation, and an incredible oneness with you."

God wants us to look for signs, not in a demanding way ("God, give me a sign!") but in a way of exploring the ever-signing God ("God has given me signs; what are they?"). He wants us to look around and ask, "How is this sign, this event, this moment in time pointing me to You, Jesus?" The truth is, there are signs of God's love all around us every day, pointing us to Jesus.

What signs of God's love have you noticed around you?

Signs of God's love are everywhere. They are tangible and abundant. They are before us. I hope you will once again taste and see that the Lord is good!

Talk with God

Abundantly loving God, thank You for pouring out Your love through Your Son, Jesus Christ. Open my eyes and ears today so I can taste and see Your goodness to me. Also, as I look around me at people who are dry and thirsty, help me to be a sign of Your goodness and love poured outward to them today. Amen.

DAY 3: THE GIFT OF DESPERATION

Read God's Word

³"Blessed are the poor in spirit, for theirs is the kingdom of heaven.

⁴"Blessed are those who mourn, for they will be comforted.

⁵"Blessed are the meek, for they will inherit the earth.

⁶"Blessed are those who hunger and thirst for righteousness, for they will be filled.

⁷"Blessed are the merciful, for they will receive mercy.

⁸"Blessed are the pure in heart, for they will see God.

⁹"Blessed are the peacemakers, for they will be called children of God.

¹⁰"Blessed are those who are persecuted for righteousness' sake, for theirs is the kingdom of heaven.

¹¹"Blessed are you when people revile you and persecute you and utter all kinds of evil against you falsely on my account. ¹²Rejoice and be glad, for your reward is great in heaven, for in the same way they persecuted the prophets who were before you."

(Matthew 5:3-12)

Reflect and Respond

Despite what movies would have you believe, teenage romances are not the stuff dreams are made of. There's a lot of awkwardness, embarrassment, and tongue-tied self-consciousness. I remember playing matchmaker in high school after I learned that one of my friends had a deep and abiding love for one of our male classmates, a passion that stood the test of time (which for us was at least two to three class periods if not an entire school day). She sent me over to talk to the object of her affection with the standard instructions: "Find out if he likes me, but don't let him know that I like him."

I crossed the lunchroom to his table and casually brought up her name in conversation. At once I noticed his cheeks flush and his speech start to stutter with the endearing awkwardness of a teenage boy in love (or at least deep like). He confessed he had been interested in her for weeks! This was great news. However, he sent me back only after I made a solemn promise that I wouldn't reveal his feelings. "I like her, but I don't want her to know how much I like her. That would ruin it," he said.

The impasse was due to one thing: neither of them wanted to seem desperate. Desperation meant admitting that you had a desire or need for the other person, and somehow that made you less desirable. But if a relationship was ever going to get beyond the stage of glances across English class, someone was going to have to get desperate enough to admit interest in the other person.

Desperation isn't a popular state of being. No one wants to be the last girl without a date for prom when all her friends have been asked, the person

Desperation isn't a preferred or pleasant condition, but it's the stuff that miracles are made of.

sending a hundredth resume for jobs he or she really needs, the guy on the corner with the sign that says "Anything will help."

Desperation isn't a preferred or pleasant condition, but it's the stuff that miracles are made of.

What do you think is the connection between miracles and desperation?

When I began the quest to "figure out" the miracles of Jesus in the New Testament (and in the process, the misguided attempt to "figure out" the God behind the miracles), I read through the Gospels with a pencil in my hand. Next to every miracle I found, I wrote an "M" in the margin. "M" marked the spot of the treasure I was looking for, the place where God's power broke through into this world in visible and dramatic ways. But when I looked back at all the M's in the margins, I noticed a pattern in those stories. Right before each M I found desperation: a person or group of people who were at the end of their rope and had no hope unless Jesus stepped in to fix their situation.

Think about it. Miracles are for desperate people. If you're not desperate, why would you need a miracle? In each miracle story, someone comes to the end of available choices—running out of ideas, options, strength, and resources—and Jesus steps in to make things right. Desperation always precedes a miracle.

I found that I had been so busy focusing on Jesus in these stories—perhaps the way one watches a magician carefully to figure out how he's doing the trick—that I had missed the other half of the equation completely: the someone that the miracle was for. And that someone was desperate.

Read the following Scriptures. In the column on the left, write a word or phrase from each that sums up the person's powerlessness and desperation. In the column on the right, name the miracle that follows.

Desperation Description	Miracle
Mark 7:25-26	
Mark 9:17-18, 24	
Luke 18:35-38	
John 5:1-9	
John 11:21	

Think about it: someone is blind, or lame, or dead. Someone's child is sick, or dying, or demon possessed. Thousands of people are hungry, and there's not enough to feed them. A boat full of people is about to capsize. Ten people are walking around with leprosy, outcast from their families and community. A woman is bent over. A man's hand is withered beyond recognition. A woman has been bleeding for twelve years. A child is dead.

Jesus is the miracle worker of those in despair, the Savior of desperate people.

Along with the M's in the margin for miracle, I began to add a D for desperation. And as I looked through this pattern, finding desperation answered by miracle again and again, I made an exciting discovery.

First, let's review quickly. Read John 2:11 in the margin and recall the two purposes of miracles that we considered in Day 1. Complete the statements below:

Miracles reveal God's _____.

Miracles cultivate _____ in God.

What I discovered was a new way of looking at God's glory. What if the glory of God is not just about the majestic, powerful acts that draw our attention but also about the specific people and situations God uses that power to help—which also cultivate our belief? So...

God's glory = God's power and might.

AND

God's glory = God's direction of that power and might to serve the desperate, downtrodden, and marginalized.

This phenomenon of God's special attention for those at the bottom rung of society isn't limited to the miracle accounts. Again and again in Scripture God turns the tables on our understanding of what it means to be blessed by God. When we say "I am so blessed," we usually mean a state of prosperity, health, and comfort. But reading the Sermon on the Mount turns this upside down.

In this amazing teaching in Matthew 5, Jesus rattles off a list of the types of people He sees as blessed, which we have come to call the Beatitudes. Instead of the prosperous and comfortable, we find a whole different kind of blessedness.

Jesus is the miracle worker of those in despair, the Savior of desperate people.

Jesus did this, the first of his signs, in Cana of Galilee, and revealed his glory; and his disciples believed in him.

(John 2:11)

Reread Matthew 5:3-11 and note below those who are blessed:

How do these descriptions of "blessed" differ from what the world calls "blessed"?

> **In God's economy, the poor in spirit, those in mourning, the meek, the persecuted, and those who are insulted and falsely accused are *blessed*.**

In God's economy, the poor in spirit, those in mourning, the meek, the persecuted, and those who are insulted and falsely accused are *blessed*. Even the celebrated "Blessed are the peacemakers," which is so often quoted from this list, means that those who are blessed to make peace actually are those who find themselves at the center of conflict, struggle, and war.

Why are these folks, whom we normally would view with pity, blessed? Because they know their need for God. Those of us who are still pretending we can get through life in our own strength don't often turn to God and ask for help. If God loves to bless the desperate, reach the broken, and heal those who come to Him with their wounds, then the brokenness that causes us to cry out to Him actually can be considered a blessing. The entire Beatitudes can be summed up in the phrase "Blessed are the desperate, for they shall seek God and find Him."

How is desperation a gift from God?

Desperation is a gift from God because it teaches us we can't do this on our own. Every time we say to ourselves, "I can make it on my own," we are fooling ourselves, wearing a mask of self-reliance and believing a lie of self-subsistence. We're all, every one of us, badly in need of Jesus' help, but the truth is that it's only the desperate who go looking for it. And they are the ones who receive.

When have you found yourself in a desperate situation? How did life's circumstances force you to stop pretending that you could do it all on your own?

How did Jesus help you in your desperation?

Desperation is the gift of not being able to pretend anymore. It's the hard things that send us running into God's open arms.

After going on my treasure hunt through the Gospels for the M for miracles and then for the D for desperate that always preceded it, there were two miracles that confused me—confounded me, even. I couldn't quite locate the desperation in them. We will look at one of them later in our study, but the other was the very first miracle we are exploring this week, when Jesus turned water into wine.

Review the story of the wedding at Cana in John 2:1-12 (see page 17). How would you describe the scene?

Where was the desperation here? A party was going on. They ran out of wine, and Jesus gave them a divine and abundant refill. Party on!

If we look at this miracle without understanding the back story, it almost seems Jesus is performing a party trick for the disciples: "Hey guys! Look at this!" But we need to remember that this was a wedding in a first-century, not a twenty-first century, context.

First of all, theirs was not a convenience culture—no sending someone running to the store for more to drink. Second, the wedding lasted a week or more, and wine was the main beverage for the guests. Finally, the social context in which this happened meant that it was no little faux pas but a major disaster.

Timothy Keller says that "this was not a mere breach of etiquette but a social and psychological catastrophe, particularly in a traditional honor-and-shame culture."[4] An honor-and-shame culture was one in which every social act brought either honor or shame to your family, your clan. Every individual represented a family, and so any good or kind act from one individual to another meant that there was a positive exchange; and the other family would owe them something in return (a reciprocal invitation or gift). A negative transaction, on the other hand, could bring shame that would last for generations.

A family essentially entered a social contract with other families when they invited them to a feast, promising to provide for their needs. So if they broke that contract by running out of wine, the groom and his family actually could be sued by the guests![5]

> Desperation is the gift of not being able to pretend anymore. It's the hard things that send us running into God's open arms.

Here we have the most important event of a young couple's life. They are being introduced to life in the community that they will depend on for trade and commerce, support, social and religious community, and even future marriages of their children. If they get off on the wrong foot—and running out of wine is possibly the worst—they could be, at best, the subject of the village's jests for years[6] or, at worst, social pariahs cut off from the benefits of society in a day when all of your supplies for living came from community, not commerce.

This was a desperate situation. This family was facing certain shame and guilt.

Read John 2:7-9 again (page 17). How did Jesus rescue them?

Instead of a party trick, we see an introduction to what we will come to recognize as Jesus' specialty: using His power for the powerless and helpless to eliminate shame and guilt. Not only did He prevent certain disaster but He also turned a desperate situation into an abundant blessing.

Look again at John 2:9-10 (page 17). In what way did Jesus do even more than was necessary? How do we see abundance here?

Jesus not only turned the water into wine—He turned it into the *best* wine! And there was more than enough for everyone.

The place that they ran out is the place where they ran into Jesus, and it ended up being the best thing that could have happened. We will see this happen again and again as we look at the people in desperate need in the miracle stories of Jesus.

When we find ourselves in situations that could bring shame and guilt, we recognize that Jesus is the rescuer of desperate people. The only way to a deep connection with the powerful Christ of the miracles is first to encounter our deep need for Him. If we think we can enjoy His power without first admitting our own powerlessness, we are mistaken.

If you or someone you love is in a desperate situation today, take heart. When you find yourself in a place where you run out of your own strength, that is precisely the place you may run into Jesus!

Talk with God

Jesus, forgive me for living as if I could do life in my own strength. Thank You for the moments when I've found myself at the end of my rope and needing Your help and strength. Today I pray

When you find yourself in a place where you run out of your own strength, that is precisely the place you may run into Jesus!

for those in desperate situations. May You use everything at Your disposal, including me, to show them mercy and love. Amen.

DAY 4: THE TALK OF THE WEDDING

Read God's Word

³When the wine gave out, the mother of Jesus said to him, "They have no wine." ⁴And Jesus said to her, "Woman, what concern is that to you and to me? My hour has not yet come." ⁵His mother said to the servants, "Do whatever he tells you." ⁶Now standing there were six stone water jars for the Jewish rites of purification, each holding twenty or thirty gallons. ⁷Jesus said to them, "Fill the jars with water." And they filled them up to the brim. ⁸He said to them, "Now draw some out, and take it to the chief steward." So they took it.

(John 2:3-8)

Reflect and Respond

I walked into a night class I had signed up for and sat down in a group of strangers, excited to improve my writing skills and meet and learn from other writers. The teacher began by handing out index cards and asking us to write our names and an answer to the question "Why did you sign up to take a class in writing fiction?" My pen hovered over the card for what seemed like an eternity, and then I finally wrote. "I didn't know I signed up for a fiction class. I write nonfiction. I'm here by mistake."

I came close to leaving at the break and never returning, but I stayed. And I'm so glad that I did. I learned more from the lessons in writing fiction about how to write the truth than I ever imagined I could. One of the hardest lessons of the class was on writing dialogue. I never imagined that writing convincing conversation could be so incredibly difficult. The teacher explained that it is difficult to capture different points of view on paper, to put words in other people's mouths in a way that sounds natural and believable. I'll never forget what he added: "To write good dialogue, you need to understand where each person is coming from; and they may be in a very different place and time than you are. You need to know them inside and out, to know their world and their heart, in order to write their words."

At the heart of the story of Jesus turning water into wine during a wedding at Cana is a conversation between Jesus and his mother, Mary. This dialogue may be one of the most misunderstood in the Bible, since so many people read it without taking time to understand Jesus and Mary inside and out, both their world and their hearts.

It's always tempting to read Scripture from our own cultural perspective. One reason we study the Bible is to discover what life and culture were like at the time the stories in Scripture occurred in order to understand the original intent of the author. Once we know what the stories meant for their original audience, we can better know what they mean for us now.

If we read the conversation between Jesus and his mother through our own cultural lens, we may end up a little shocked. Mary could seem bossy and unrelenting. Jesus could sound resentful and adolescent. One might wonder how the Son of God could speak to his own mother in such a tone—the same tone I might refer to when telling my kids, "Don't take that *tone* with me!" Let's read through their conversation in two different ways: hearing it from our own cultural understanding today, and then hearing it from theirs.

"They have no wine."

Based on your own cultural understanding, how would you interpret these words of Mary in John 2:3?

Today's cultural understanding might lead us to hear Mary's statement with the same tone a mother might use to say, "Your socks are in the middle of the floor." It's a statement that's not really a statement but a passive-aggressive request or demand.

But as we've learned this week, wine had a much deeper significance in their culture. You'll remember that it was a sign of joy because it signified the coming of the Messiah. If wine is a sign that God was showing up in power and love to save His people, imagine what the absence of wine would mean.

Read Isaiah 24:7-11 below. This passage depicts a hurting nation longing for God to send the Messiah, the One who will come and save them. Circle any mentions of wine or a lack of wine.

⁷The wine dries up,

the vine languishes,

all the merry-hearted sigh.

⁸The mirth of the timbrels is stilled,

the noise of the jubilant has ceased,

the mirth of the lyre is stilled.

⁹No longer do they drink wine with singing;

strong drink is bitter to those who drink it.

¹⁰*The city of chaos is broken down,*
   every house is shut up so that no one can enter.
¹¹*There is an outcry in the streets for lack of wine;*
   all joy has reached its eventide;
   the gladness of the earth is banished.

A dry and thirsty people—merrymakers who had run out of wine—would signify that people were longing, thirsty, ready for God to come and save them. So when Mary said, "They have no wine," she was essentially saying, "Look, Jesus. They are longing for the Messiah!" What a beautiful sign of God's people being ready to receive Him.

As a mother—and one who had received miraculous messages about her son before he was ever born—Mary had kept a close eye on Jesus his entire life. Lately she had seen Jesus' ministry emerging: his baptism by his cousin John and his calling of disciples to follow Him. Now she was likely wondering if this sign, the wine running out, meant that it was time for Jesus to step into a more public role.

How does this insight into the biblical and cultural context enrich your understanding of this scene?

Consider what we've learned about desperation and miracles. It's a gift to admit failure, want, and lack, because ultimately it brings us to rely on God's help. Now notice that Mary is the only one willing to point out the desperate situation at this wedding. This is a beautiful situation where a people in need of help are connected with the One who has the power to help, not only with their need for wine but also with their need for God's intervention in their lives. Mary is a hero in this story, not a nag.

"Woman, what concern is that to you and to me?"

Based on your own cultural understanding, how would you interpret these words of Jesus in John 2:4?

Our cultural understanding today might leave us shocked by the blatant disrespect in Jesus' words. Just picture yourself addressing your own mother or a woman in a position of authority as "*Woman!*" "Woman, make me dinner!" "Woman, what are you talking about?" That kind of talk would not go over well in my family, and probably not in yours either. But in Jesus' culture, addressing someone with the word *woman* was a sign of respect—similar to someone today calling a woman "Ma'am" out of respect.

When you study the Bible and come across a word that is confusing or that stands out in some way, it's always best to start by seeing the other ways that particular book uses the word. So let's look at the other places in John's Gospel where Jesus begins a sentence with the word *woman*.

In John 4, Jesus converses respectfully with a woman who, according to the culture, would be beneath Him in every way because she was female and a Samaritan, and she had been married several times.

Read John 4:21 in the margin. What was Jesus talking with this woman about? How does knowing the cultural usage of the word *woman* affect your understanding of Jesus' dialogue with her?

Jesus said to her, "Woman, believe me, the hour is coming when you will worship the Father neither on this mountain nor in Jerusalem."

(John 4:21)

Most men would have avoided talking with this fallen woman altogether, but Jesus engaged her in a theological dialogue as an equal, showing her kindness. "Woman, believe me..."

In John 8, Jesus addressed a woman who had been shamed by other men when they caught her in the act of adultery.

Read John 8:10-11 in the margin. How did Jesus treat this woman? What did He tell her?

[10]"Woman, where are they? Has no one condemned you?"[11] She said, "No one, sir." And Jesus said, "Neither do I condemn you. Go your way, and from now on do not sin again."

(John 8:10-11)

Instead of condemning the woman caught in adultery, Jesus addressed her with kindness, compassion, and gentle instruction. "Woman, where are they?"

In John 20, we find the risen Jesus speaking with Mary Magdalene.

Read John 20:15 in the margin. What did Jesus ask?

Jesus said to her, "Woman, why are you weeping? Whom are you looking for?" Supposing him to be the gardener, she said to him, "Sir, if you have carried him away, tell me where you have laid him, and I will take him away."

(John 20:15)

Here Jesus used the word *woman* with tenderness to address a grieving Mary Magdalene crying at his tomb. "Woman, why are you weeping?"

There is only one other place in the Gospel of John where Jesus addresses His *mother* as "woman," and it is a very tender moment.

Read John 19:26-27 in the margin. As Jesus is dying on the cross, what tone do you imagine Him using to speak to His mother and best friend?

What look do you imagine on His face?

[26]When Jesus saw his mother and the disciple whom he loved standing beside her, he said to his mother, "Woman, here is your son." [27]Then he said to the disciple, "Here is your mother." And from that hour the disciple took her into his own home.

(John 19:26-27)

We see from these examples that Jesus' interaction with women was always respectful. He always engaged them as equal conversation partners, showing respect and kindness. The conversation at the wedding is part of a pattern of lovingly addressing women in a culture that did not value their worth.

"My hour has not yet come."

Based on your own cultural understanding, how would you interpret these words of Jesus in John 2:4?

Today's cultural understanding might cause us to hear Jesus saying that He's not ready. It's not yet the hour to begin His ministry. But if we read these words with the rest of the Gospel of John in mind, we might see that "my hour" is a different kind of reference.

When Mary brings up Jesus' Messiahship by referring to the people's lack of wine, He reminds her that His hour has not yet come. When *will* His hour come? To answer that, let's go to the garden of Gethsemane.

Read John 17:12 in the margin, Jesus' words spoken in agony of prayer. What is the hour that Jesus is referring to that is quickly approaching? (See John 19.)

"While I was with them, I protected them in your name that you have given me. I guarded them, and not one of them was lost except the one destined to be lost, so that the scripture might be fulfilled."

(John 17:12)

The final hour when mercy and sacrifice will flow liberally will involve the death and resurrection of Jesus. Jesus knows that the thirst for Messiah, echoed in the thirst for wine, will be answered only in His own death and resurrection. He's not speaking of "the hour" as the start of His ministry but as the final culmination.

Listening for instruction and then doing God's will means that we're putting the whole messy situation in God's hands, acknowledging we are simply the servants of His will.

"*Do whatever he tells you.*"

How might someone interpret these words from John 2:5?

An untrained eye of a contemporary reader might see a nagging mother who just won't give up on her ideas of what her son should be doing. But students of the Bible can see deeper. This phrase is one of absolute trust in Jesus' authority. Mary didn't tell the servants or Jesus what to do; she pointed them to obey the One with great authority in the room.

This is good advice for us too. Whatever Jesus says to do, we should do. It might look impossible or foolish. It might be hard and thankless work. But listening for instruction and then doing God's will means that we're putting the whole messy situation in God's hands, acknowledging we are simply the servants of His will.

What is something Jesus has asked you to do recently? Have you responded in obedience, or are you dragging your feet? Explain your response.

Dialogue is tough! I learned that lesson the hard way in what I thought was the wrong writing class. In the end, it taught me to pay close attention to words, as well as the culture and heart behind them.

When we see the heart of God, we find that He wants to dialogue with us—to share His heart of love for us and His instructions for living a life of holiness and wholeness. I hope that you've learned something from Jesus' words today, and that you will take time to enter into your own conversation with Him now.

Talk with God

Lord, teach me to pray. I want to talk to You and hear Your voice. I want to know Your heart and do Your will. Speak to me now, Lord. With Your help, I will do whatever You tell me to do. (Spend a few moments in quiet listening.) Amen.

DAY 5: "DO WHATEVER HE TELLS YOU"

Read God's Word

⁵His mother said to the servants, "Do whatever he tells you."

⁶Nearby stood six stone water jars, the kind used by the Jews for ceremonial washing, each holding from twenty to thirty gallons.

⁷Jesus said to the servants, "Fill the jars with water"; so they filled them to the brim.

⁸Then he told them, "Now draw some out and take it to the master of the banquet."

They did so.

(John 2:5-8 NIV)

¹⁶Then the eleven disciples went to Galilee, to the mountain where Jesus had told them to go. ¹⁷When they saw him, they worshiped him; but some doubted. ¹⁸Then Jesus came to them and said, "All authority in heaven and on earth has been given to me. ¹⁹Therefore go and make disciples of all nations, baptizing them in the name of the Father and of the Son and of the Holy Spirit, ²⁰and teaching them to obey everything I have commanded you. And surely I am with you always, to the very end of the age."

(Matthew 28:16-20 NIV)

Reflect and Respond

A good friend who loves mission work has made several trips to visit an orphanage in India. Each time she goes, the woman who is the head of the orphanage—called "Ma" by the kids who live there—asks the new American visitors to go through a cultural orientation when they first arrive. Life is different in India, and we have habits that are second nature to us but that might cause friction or offense there. Visitors generally want to be considerate and respectful during their stay, so they try to observe customs such as covering their shoulders and legs, even in hot weather, or making an effort to use their right hand when eating or greeting others, since the left hand is reserved for unsavory functions in that culture.

But my friend the traveler reports there is one rule that is hard for Americans to keep, and it has to do with their relationship with the children in the orphanage. While the American visitors are talking with or playing with the children, sometimes their "Ma" or another adult in authority will call them away, announcing that it's time to study, go to bed, help with chores, or clean up from a meal. The American visitors often say something such as, "Let's just finish this game we're playing" or "Finish telling me your story and then go." That doesn't seem like a cultural faux pas to us, but it is. In India, children are taught that "slow obedience is no obedience" and they must do as they're told as soon as they are told, or it's an act of disobedience. So, if they are swayed by a fun-loving visitor inviting them to take another turn at a game, they often get in trouble once they finally respond to the task they've been asked to do. Obedience is a necessity in their culture, and obeying immediately and without question is just as important as the obedience itself.

When I contrast this example with the speed of obedience I often witness from my own kids, it's a bit staggering! They're pretty great kids, but I am sure some of their earliest counting skills came from the fact that I so often had to tell them more than twice to obey and then threaten with "One, two, three…!" Obedience is a value most parents try to instill in their children, but the understanding of how quickly that obedience should happen varies from culture to culture and household to household.

We are often drawn to the miracle stories because of the power of an omnipotent God on display in His mighty acts. But in addition to His power, there is a quieter character on display in the miracles: our obedience.

Reread John 2:5-8. What did Mary ask the servants to do?

What did Jesus ask them to do?

Let's think about the servants at the wedding banquet for a moment. This celebration was obviously a huge workload for these servants. Feeding and serving all of these additional guests for a multiple-day—possibly multiple-week—party meant that they had been working overtime to provide for the needs of the guests. They were probably the first ones to notice that the wine had run out, and they even may have felt anxious that they would be blamed when the next guest ordered a refill and they had to tell them there was no wine. One thing was certain: wine is not something that could be quickly manufactured or made.

Then one of the party guests pointed to her son and spoke those iconic words: "Do whatever he tells you." This statement is the blank check of obedience. Who knew what this new teacher would command? When He did speak, it certainly was out of the ordinary.

Just imagine the conversation between servants as they rushed back to the kitchen.

Servant 1: "He wants us to go get the WHAT? Those jars aren't for weddings; they aren't even for holding drink; those are for religious purification ceremonies!"

Servant 2: "I know! And He wants us to serve WHAT to the wedding guests? The master will certainly be a laughingstock if we serve up water in jars intended for a religious ritual when the people are expecting more wine. Who is this guy anyway?"

I can only imagine the stressed expressions of the servants as they anticipated the angry look on the face of the master of the banquet when they dipped a cup for tasting into a jar they had just filled with water. Perhaps when things went wrong, it was the servants who took the blame—and sometimes the beating. For whatever reason, they were willing to obey the stranger's strange instructions.

The servants discovered that obedience isn't easy work.

Look again at John 2:7. How did the servants carry out Jesus' instruction? Complete the sentence below:

They filled them to the _____.

They obeyed fully, hauling enough water to fill six large jars. No slacking; no room for doubt that someone had added anything other than water to the jars.

Here's one thing I noticed when writing my M's in the margins of my Bible to indicate where a miracle occurred: I wasn't sure of the exact moment when this particular miracle occurred. I couldn't tell if the water changed while the jars were being filled, or when a ladle was dipped into the water, or even when the cup was lifted to the lips of the master of the banquet. I hovered over the margin for a moment trying to decide where the M belonged, because the Bible isn't clear on this point. But if anyone knew when that moment happened, if anyone witnessed the miraculous transformation taking place, it had to be the servants.

Review John 2:8-10. What did Jesus tell the servants to do with the wine?

What do we learn from verse 9?

Extra Insight

Each water jar would have held twenty to thirty gallons each (see John 2:6).

Because of their obedience, the servants had a front-row seat to God's power on display. The steward or master was confused when he drank the wine, not knowing where it came from, and the others at the party might have drawn their own conclusions about when and how the new and improved wine appeared; but the servants saw the miracle in action. They knew the truth. In a way, Jesus was actually giving the servants something that not even the honored guests or even the master of the party knew: they were receiving firsthand knowledge of Jesus' power. Though this is the first miracle that Jesus performed publicly, it's not very public because only the servants are let in on the secret.

It's amazing how often obedience is an essential ingredient of a miracle. Finding the small acts of human obedience that are a part of God's miracles may not always be as exciting as looking for the mind-blowing results of God's actions, but it shows us how He loves to work in relationship with His people. Let's look at a few examples together.

How did God use something Moses already had in each of these miraculous events?

Exodus 14:21

Exodus 17:5-6

Exodus 17:9-10

God never simply said, "Hey, Moses, watch this." Instead He told him to stretch out his hand to part the Red Sea, strike a rock with his staff to produce water, and raise his staff in the air to be victorious in battle. God often uses some gift or resource we already possess as the catalyst for a miracle when we put what is in our hands in His hands.

When has God used a gift or resource of yours to bring about extraordinary results?

Naaman, who sought healing from God for a terrible and isolating skin disease, is another example. In his desperation, he even traveled to another nation to find a prophet who could tell him what to do. But he balked when the instructions included dipping himself seven times in an "inferior" river.

> It's amazing how often obedience is an essential ingredient of a miracle.

> God often uses some gift or resource we already possess as the catalyst for a miracle when we put what is in our hands in His hands.

Read 2 Kings 5:14 in the margin. What did Naaman eventually do, and what happened as a result?

Only when Naaman was obedient, doing something he considered beneath him, did his healing occur.

God is always on the side of restoration and wholeness, but He calls us to participate in our own healing by obeying Him. Our internal lives often need as much or more healing than our bodies, and obedience to God often brings healing to both. We'll see this again and again in the healing miracles of Jesus (stay tuned for Week 4).

When has your obedience, or the obedience of someone else, played a part in bringing about healing or restoration?

In addition to the healing miracles, we see obedience playing a role in many of Jesus' miracles.

Look up each Scripture and complete the chart below:

Scripture	Act of Obedience	Miracle
John 5:1-8		
John 6:1-13		
John 21:1-6		

In each of these instances, an act of obedience was required for a miraculous outcome. God often calls us to act in faith, trusting that He will meet our needs. And prayer is generally a part of this process. In fact, prayer is obedience. Those who pray in desperation and then see God's answers unfold have a front-row seat to God at work, while others may tend to view amazing outcomes as coincidence. Mary certainly had a front-row seat to God's miraculous power. It's no accident that Mary is the one who instructed the servants to do whatever Jesus told them to do. Her own story is a witness to the miracles that often follow obedience.

He went down and immersed himself seven times in the Jordan, according to the word of the man of God; his flesh was restored like the flesh of a young boy, and he was clean.

(2 Kings 5:14)

Those who pray in desperation and then see God's answers unfold have a front-row seat to God at work, while others may tend to view amazing outcomes as coincidence.

Read Luke 1:26-38. What news did the angel bring Mary?

What question did she ask? (v. 34)

What was her ultimate response? (v. 38)

As an unmarried teenage girl, an angel told Mary that she would become pregnant and give birth to the Son of God. Though she wondered how this would be accomplished, since she was a virgin, her response was one of obedience: "May it be done to me according to your word" (Luke 1:38 NASB).

Contrast Mary's example to that of her relative's husband, Zechariah. While she was of low status (female, young, unmarried, and poor) he was of high status—male, older, married, and of the priestly class. Yet when told in a similar manner that his aging and barren wife, Elizabeth, would have a son (John the Baptist), Zechariah responded differently.

Read Luke 1:18-20. What did Zechariah ask, and what does his question reveal?

What did the angel say would happen as a result of Zechariah's response?

Zechariah was struck dumb until his son was born, but Mary was blessed with affirmation when she went to visit Elizabeth.

Read Luke 1:39-56. What happened when Elizabeth heard Mary's greeting? (v. 41)

What affirmation did Elizabeth give Mary? (vv. 42-45)

How did Mary respond, and how does this further demonstrate her obedience? (vv. 46-55)

Mary is known as an icon of obedience, for she not only gave birth to Jesus "according to God's word" but also raised Him and witnessed His death and resurrection. It's no wonder she identified with the servants at the wedding in Cana and reminded them to "do whatever He tells you." She lived by those words, being obedient to God.

A life of full obedience is what God desires from each of us. It won't always be easy, but it is always our best choice.

What would full obedience to God look like in your life right now? What do you sense Him calling you to do?

Here's the thing about recognizing the relationship between our obedience and God's miracles: it keeps us dependent on God. Rather than the kind of white-knuckled, teeth-gritted determination that results from believing that we obey God by acting alone and in our strength, we see our actions as part of God's work, remembering that God's power is at work in and through us. By obeying God, we are playing a part in His grander plans. It also keeps us from becoming detached spectators of God's work in the world.

If we approach miracles thinking God will "knock our socks off" by doing all the work Himself, we miss the point. God wants to involve each of us in the plan for His kingdom to come here on earth as it is in heaven. If you would like a front-row seat to see God at work and be part of the amazing transformation of the world we live in, put on a servant's uniform and "do whatever he tells you."

Talk with God

Loving God, I am desperate for You and dependent on You. I want nothing more than to be Your servant, following Your will and learning Your ways. Help me to remember that Your power at work in me can do amazing things. Forgive me when I try to go it alone, relying on my own effort. Continue showing me that You are a miracle-working God. Amen.

A life of full obedience is what God desires from each of us. It won't always be easy, but it is always our best choice.

If you would like a front row-seat to see God at work and be part of the amazing transformation of the world we live in, put on a servant's uniform and "do whatever he tells you."

VIDEO VIEWER GUIDE: WEEK 1

In the Gospels, where Jesus is involved, _desperation_ always precedes a miracle.

When we ___run out___ is when we are most likely to run to ___Jesus___.

John 2:1-5

The first thing we have to do with our desperation is ___acknowledge___ it.

Our desperation points us to our ___need___, but it really points us to ___Jesus___.

The place where you are running out is the primary place you're going to see Jesus' ___power___.

Isaiah 24:7

Isaiah 25:6

It doesn't matter if our dreams or moments of desperation are ___small___; God's answer is ___Big___.

Week 2

THE MIRACLE OF ABUNDANCE

From Our Little, Jesus Makes Much

DAY 1: THE POWER OF THE SMALL

Read God's Word

30The apostles gathered around Jesus and reported to him all they had done and taught. 31Then, because so many people were coming and going that they did not even have a chance to eat, he said to them, "Come with me by yourselves to a quiet place and get some rest."

32So they went away by themselves in a boat to a solitary place. 33But many who saw them leaving recognized them and ran on foot from all the towns and got there ahead of them. 34When Jesus landed and saw a large crowd, he had compassion on them, because they were like sheep without a shepherd. So he began teaching them many things.

35By this time it was late in the day, so his disciples came to him. "This is a remote place," they said, "and it's already very late. 36Send the people away so that they can go to the surrounding countryside and villages and buy themselves something to eat."

37But he answered, "You give them something to eat."

They said to him, "That would take more than half a year's wages! Are we to go and spend that much on bread and give it to them to eat?"

38"How many loaves do you have?" he asked. "Go and see."

When they found out, they said, "Five—and two fish."

39Then Jesus directed them to have all the people sit down in groups on the green grass. 40So they sat down in groups of hundreds and fifties. 41Taking the five loaves and the two fish and looking up to heaven, he gave thanks and broke the loaves. Then he gave them to his disciples to distribute to the people. He also divided the two fish among them all. 42They all ate and were satisfied, 43and the disciples picked up twelve basketfuls of broken pieces of bread and fish. 44The number of the men who had eaten was five thousand.

(Mark 6:30-44 NIV)

Reflect and Respond

God loves to deal in the small. I know that sounds like a contradiction in a study about miracles, where we step back in awe of the big and bold actions of God, but it's true. The big things that God does often begin with something small. Let's begin our week on miracles of abundance by looking at some small things that shaped some big outcomes.

Read the following verses and note how small things were used in a big way.

1 Samuel 17:48-50

David + Goliath

1 Kings 18:41-46

Cloud → storm

1 Kings 19:11-13

Elijah hears God in silence

Matthew 13:31-32

✳ *mustard seed*

James 3:5

tongue is powerful

Little David conquers Goliath with just a small stone (1 Samuel 17:48-50). A minuscule cloud signifies the beginning of a great storm the prophet Elijah predicted (1 Kings 18:41-46). Elijah hears God in the sound of sheer silence, not the earthquake, fire, or wind (1 Kings 19:11-13). Jesus points to a tiny mustard seed as the representation of true faith, since it starts out small but grows large (Matthew 13:31-32). James indicates that the tongue is powerful and mighty, reminding us that a small spark can ignite a forest fire (James 3:5 NIV).

Where there's a scarcity of ingredients, it reminds us that it's God's power, not human ingenuity or provision, to which we should give our attention and praise. The harder the odds and the smaller the resources, the more amazed we are when God pulls through and makes something amazing out of almost nothing.

No miracle exemplifies this quite as well as the day Jesus fed a crowd of five thousand. As the narrative begins we discover the disciples are already run down. They are tired and worn out from ministering to others, and they've been so busy they haven't even had a chance to eat. I'm sure you've felt like this from time to time, when your responsibilities and care for others have drained you so much that you are desperately in need of time just to care for yourself.

Jesus invites the disciples to come to a quiet place where they can rest. They cross over to the other side of the lake in a boat, but people hurry by foot to get there ahead of them, so that when they arrive another great crowd has already formed (Mark 6:33). This helps us understand the crowds that are gathering around Jesus during His ministry, especially around the Sea of Galilee. This is

The harder the odds and the smaller the resources, the more amazed we are when God pulls through and makes something amazing out of almost nothing.

not a very large region, and the towns are not very far apart; so when people witness the amazing things Jesus is doing, they tell their friends and rush ahead to the next town where they can find Him.

When Jesus, who is still tired and hungry from His ministry in the previous town, arrives, He encounters a crowd—described as "great" in size.

Reread Mark 6:34. Why does Jesus have compassion on them, rather than being frustrated or put out?

Here's the story's first mention of scarcity. Jesus notices first that they are starving for leadership, teaching, and truth, so He "began teaching them many things" (Mark 6:34 NIV). Then, at the end of a long day of teaching, the disciples call Jesus' attention to another kind of scarcity in the situation.

Reread Mark 6:35-37 and answer the following questions.

What do the disciples emphasize about the hour and location?

What do they want Jesus to do?

What does Jesus tell them to do?

It seems a bit strange to complain to a limitless God about how impossible your situation is, but that's what the disciples are doing. In fact, our prayers sometimes sound this way too; we lay our desperate situations out before the King of kings and tell Him just how impossible things look to us.

When have you laid out your scarcity or shortage before God in desperation, showing Him just how impossible things look?

Let's review all the scarcity and shortage emphasized throughout the story so far. The disciples are exhausted and hungry, the crowds are "great" in size but lack a shepherd to care for them, and now we find that thousands of people are hungry. When Jesus tells the disciples to take inventory, they find themselves digging in their pockets for crumbs!

8Another of his disciples, Andrew, Simon Peter's brother, spoke up, 9"Here is a boy with five small barley loaves and two small fish, but how far will they go among so many?"

(John 6:8-9)

Even though we're looking at the story from the point of view of the Gospel of Mark today—and we'll consider accounts of the story in other Gospels tomorrow—I'd like to go ahead and mention one small detail found only in John's telling of this story.

Read John 6:8-9 in the margin. What small thing does Andrew mention?

small boy

I mentioned that this was a "small" detail because we're talking here about things that are small in our eyes but great in Jesus' hands. The small thing mentioned here in John is, of course, the boy. It's not a disciple who provides the small offering with which Jesus will make a miracle. It's not even an adult. It's a boy. Don't miss this: the disciples aren't even the ones with the resources here. They are totally out of food, out of ideas, and out of patience, wanting Jesus to just send everybody home so they can be done. They have nothing to offer. But the boy does.

The disciple who acts as the go-between, bringing the boy and his food to Jesus, is Andrew. Otherwise, this little one and his gifts might have been lost in the crowd. I have a personal love for the disciple Andrew because we named our son, our firstborn, Andrew. (He goes by Drew, he'll proudly tell you.)

Let's look at another time that Andrew brought someone to Jesus.

Read John 1:40-42. Who is Andrew responsible for bringing to Jesus?

40One of the two who heard John speak and followed him was Andrew, Simon Peter's brother. 41He first found his brother Simon and said to him, "We have found the Messiah" (which is translated Anointed). 42He brought Simon to Jesus, who looked at him and said, "You are Simon son of John. You are to be called Cephas" (which is translated Peter).

(John 1:40-42)

Andrew shows remarkable humility and wisdom in both of these situations. Where his brother is concerned, Andrew must know that Peter is the stronger personality and might end up getting more of Jesus' attention. (Peter is by far the most mentioned disciple, and the leader according to all four Gospels.) But he also knows that the right thing for anyone he loves is to bring him or her to Jesus. In the story of the feeding of the five thousand, Andrew knows he could be laughed at when he presents a small boy with a tiny lunch. But despite his own question regarding the sufficiency of that small amount, he must also know that any offering, no matter how small, is something great in Jesus' hands.

If there is someone in your life you're concerned about or worrying over, bring him or her to Jesus. Pray for him or her. Even that tiny act is enough for something great.

Think of a person you can bring to Jesus, and write his or her name here as an act of prayer:

Now, think of an impossible situation you've observed around you where there seems to be too little of a solution and too big of a problem, and summarize it here:

Is there a small resource that seems so small it's laughable in comparison to this great need? Bring it to Jesus now in prayer:

Our small resources in God's hands are more than enough. When blessed in Jesus' hands, the five loaves and two fish turn out to be a feast. Jesus actually divides five loaves among all of them, and then amazingly He divides the two fish among them all.

Reread Mark 6:42. What is the outcome?

The result is mind-blowing. We're told not only that everyone eats but also that *all* are satisfied! And to show that God is more than enough for all our needs: they take up leftovers, and twelve baskets are filled!

Don't miss the number here: twelve. Remember our tired and weary disciples? There are twelve of them. The number of leftover baskets helps remind them that just as they take care of the needs of others—distributing the food and giving them something to eat—God will always take care of their needs as well.

Just as in the miracle at the wedding in Cana, when there was a need to refill wine bottles and the result was an overflow of wine in large stone jars, God is always "able to do immeasurably more than all we ask or imagine" (Ephesians 3:20 NIV).

There are people who analyze this miracle in a way that implies it is no miracle at all, saying that the people just reached into their coats for the little bit of food they brought and, inspired by Jesus, began sharing generously. While generosity is indeed a gift, this text, told in all four Gospels, clearly gives

Just because miracles are impossible to understand doesn't mean they have to be impossible to believe.

us a glimpse of the awe that both the crowd and the disciples had at Jesus' miraculous actions. Just because miracles are impossible to understand doesn't mean they have to be impossible to believe. Miracles are an opportunity to marvel at the marvelous, not to explain away the unexplainable.

The crowd is large. The hunger and exhaustion are great. The boy is small. The five loaves and two fish are small. *But Jesus is enough!* Stuart Briscoe reminds us that "human resources, however limited, when willingly offered and divinely empowered, are more than adequate to achieve divine ends."[1]

Where are *you* feeling inadequate? Is there something in your own personal life or circumstances that seems too small to meet the great needs before you? Name it below, and offer your small resource(s) to Jesus. *all alone*

Remember that what is small in our hands is big in Jesus' hands. Wait with expectancy, and just see what great things He can do!

Talk with God

Lord, we all struggle with not being enough. The problems and needs of life often seem so great in comparison to what is in our grasp. I open my hands and my life to You now and ask You to do much with little. Surprise me again, Jesus. Amen.

DAY 2: BREAD OF LIFE

Read God's Word

¹Then Jesus was led by the Spirit into the wilderness to be tempted by the devil. ²After fasting forty days and forty nights, he was hungry. ³The tempter came to him and said, "If you are the Son of God, tell these stones to become bread."

⁴Jesus answered, "It is written: 'Man shall not live on bread alone, but on every word that comes from the mouth of God.'"

(Matthew 4:1-4 NIV)

³²Jesus said to them, "Very truly I tell you, it is not Moses who has given you the bread from heaven, but it is my Father who gives you the true bread from heaven. ³³For the bread of God is the bread that comes down from heaven and gives life to the world."

³⁴"Sir," they said, "always give us this bread."

35Then Jesus declared, "I am the bread of life. Whoever comes to me will never go hungry, and whoever believes in me will never be thirsty."

(John 6:32-35 NIV)

Reflect and Respond

Have you ever been part of a group that is invited to publicly share their prayer requests? Some Bible study groups, Sunday school classes, and even worship gatherings have a period where they open the floor and invite people to share their concerns and joys in prayer. While this can be an incredibly beautiful time of sharing needs and offering promises to pray, it can also make people incredibly uncomfortable.

To tell the truth, most of us don't like sharing our most vulnerable needs with others. We are sometimes afraid that it will make us seem weak or helpless to admit that we don't have our lives under control and that there are things we desperately need help, even the Lord's help, solving.

Sometimes as I sit in a circle of people sharing prayer requests, I am thinking to myself, "Which of my needs should I share and ask for prayer about? Definitely not _____ (most vulnerable area), but also not _____ (something trivial). Maybe I'll ask them to pray for _____ (something in the middle)." Aren't we humans ridiculous in our posturing to make sure we look good in one another's eyes?

Desperation is the element that breaks down our posturing. Being desperate means we know we need something that is a necessity for our lives yet is completely out of our control. In the prayer request circle, this usually begins with issues related to health. Struggles with our own health or concerns about the health of those we love are at the top of the list of things we cannot control yet want desperately to see resolved. That is why many of our initial steps of trust in sharing prayer requests begin with comments such as "Please pray for my uncle who had a stroke" or "Pray for my medical tests this week." This is a wonderful place for us to start trusting the Lord and one another with our needs, and we'll see in coming weeks that Jesus often addressed people's deep concerns about their own health and the health of their loved ones through miracles of healing, casting out evil spirits, and raising the dead.

Another level of trust in many groups is often sharing prayer requests for help with provision. This often involves requests for those searching for a new job, those concerned about discord or instability at work, or those with unexpected or overwhelming bills who are trying to make ends meet. This is another wonderful area to recognize our need before God, since all that we are and all that we have comes from Him. We tend to forget that until there is a moment when our physical needs are in danger of not being met, and then we remember to turn to Him for provision for our bellies, our bills, and our bank accounts.

> **Desperation is the element that breaks down our posturing.**

Jesus, who is the bread of life, is the One responsible for filling all our needs.

As we move into deeper levels of trust with God and with one another, we realize that Jesus, who is the bread of life, is the One responsible for filling all our needs. He reminds us of this in John 6 when He tells the disciples, "I am the bread of life. Whoever comes to me will never go hungry, and whoever believes in me will never be thirsty" (John 6:35 NIV).

Open your Bible to John 6. What story does this chapter begin with?

Now look at the teaching of Jesus in John 6:25-59, which includes one of our Scripture readings for today. As you read through these verses in your Bible, underline or circle each time Jesus mentions something that references bread, food, hunger, or eating.

The chapter opens with John's account of the miracle we studied yesterday, the feeding of the five thousand. As Jesus offers bread to hungry people, the disciples must be in awe at His ability to provide for the needs of so many with so little. Shortly afterward, a dialogue begins that's all about bread, hunger, and being filled.

Having just witnessed the miracle of the feeding of the five thousand, the disciples seem very focused on physical hunger and fullness. Jesus calls them out on this, saying, "Very truly I tell you, you are looking for me, not because you saw the signs I performed but because you ate the loaves and had your fill" (John 6:26 NIV). And in the next verse, He invites them to think about spiritual hunger: "Do not work for food that spoils, but for food that endures to eternal life" (v. 27 NIV).

Jesus' teaching goes all the way back to the forty years that their ancestors spent wandering in the wilderness and the bread that God gave them there called *manna*, which simply means "what is it?"

Reread John 6:32-34. Where does Jesus emphasize that this bread did *not* come from?

Where does He remind them that it did come from?

How do the disciples respond?

In the wilderness, God provided for their needs out of nothing; the bread simply materialized from thin air each morning. This is not unlike the nothingness the disciples encounter on the hillside with five thousand hungry people wanting bread. Mark tells us in his Gospel that Jesus asks them to take inventory of their scarcity: "'How many loaves do you have?' he asked. 'Go and see'" (Mark 6:38 NIV). They come up with next to nothing, but when they know exactly how much nothing they have, that's where His everything begins.

After the miracle, the people find Jesus on the other side of the lake and ask for this miraculous, life-giving, never-running-out bread.

Reread John 6:35. How does Jesus answer them?

Jesus responds by offering Himself—the true bread of life. Those who come to Him will never be hungry or thirsty.

God provides for all of our needs. It doesn't always make sense. We can't always figure out how He will do it. We don't always understand His methods. But He will always be there to meet our needs. God always provides.

Read Philippians 4:19 in the margin. When in your life have you witnessed God supplying your needs according to His riches?

My God will fully satisfy every need of yours according to his riches in glory in Christ Jesus.
(Philippians 4:19)

One of the most amazing parts of this miracle of providing bread and the teaching on the bread of life that follows it is that Jesus understands our hunger. He has already been faced with the same lesson the disciples are facing—the same one the Israelites in the wilderness faced—and he demonstrated trust in the provision of God. Jesus Himself has been hungry and wanted bread. He Himself was given the choice of trusting God for His provision or taking shortcuts that would mean certain physical satisfaction but spiritual failure.

At the very beginning of His ministry, immediately following His baptism, Jesus went to the wilderness to be tempted by Satan. Alone in the wilderness for forty days, Jesus was hungry—not just "I skipped breakfast" hungry but "I could eat an elephant and then order seconds" hungry. He had been fasting for forty days, and at the end of that time we're told Satan came to tempt Him to fill His belly. This tells us something about the times we are most vulnerable to

> **Times when we are hungry or lonely or tired are often the moments when our character is most tested.**

temptation. Times when we are hungry or lonely or tired are often the moments when our character is most tested.

The first temptation Satan used to challenge Jesus had to do with hunger.

Reread Matthew 4:3-4. What did Satan suggest that Jesus do?

How did Jesus respond?

Extra Insight

Jesus stayed in the wilderness for forty days struggling in the same way God's people struggled in the wilderness for forty years. A major theme of Jesus' ministry is to show He is able to succeed at the hardest parts of being human—even those where God's people had failed in the past.

Jesus had the need for bread and the power to make bread, yet He didn't use His powers to satisfy Himself. He knew that divine power was not a commodity to be used as if God's purpose is always to answer our whims. His miracles would reveal His self-giving nature, intended to satisfy others' needs, not His own.

Look up Deuteronomy 8:2-3, the passage that Jesus quoted in response to this temptation. How many years did the Israelites wander in the wilderness?

How many days was Jesus in the wilderness?

What did the Israelites learn by hungering in the wilderness and then being fed by God's manna?

When Jesus was faced with temptation, He recalled the Israelites' desert journey and remembered God's faithfulness even when they were not faithful. This is great news for us when we are tempted and fail: Jesus came to be the faithful answer to the challenges we face.

Read Hebrews 4:15 in the margin. What does this verse tell us about Jesus?

We do not have a high priest who is unable to sympathize with our weaknesses, but we have one who in every respect has been tested as we are, yet without sin.

(Hebrews 4:15)

If you find yourself tempted, tested, and tried today, stop and ask Jesus for help. He has been tempted in every way we can be, yet He resisted them all. We can trust in His goodness, faithfulness, and love.

Jesus' resistance to the temptation to create bread for His own physical hunger reveals that He would not use His power at a whim to impress others, or even feed Himself, but would use His power to meet people's deepest needs and fulfill God's purposes on earth. He denied Himself for others. This self-denying love showed up throughout His ministry. From His wilderness temptations that launched His active ministry on earth to His death on the cross that ended it, He trusted in God's provision. He knew that His Father would provide.

Mark Buchanan, a popular author and pastor, says that although many people over the years have asked for his prayers when they were facing bankruptcy and financial ruin, not one person has ever asked him to pray with them over how to invest their money. We often think of asking God for help when all of our human wisdom and resources are at an end, but we rarely realize that God wants to be intimately involved in all steps of the provision for our lives.[2]

How about you? Do you wait until desperation has you in its clutches before realizing God is right there, eager to be part of your needs, your abundance, and every aspect of your life? As you lean into prayer this week—both individually and with your group—how can you lean into the vulnerability of sharing your need for God's provision? Where we are faithful to look to Him, He will always provide.

> This is great news for us when we are tempted and fail: Jesus came to be the faithful answer to the challenges we face.

Talk with God

Dear God, I am tempted every day to be self-sufficient, trying to provide for all my own needs and resisting the vulnerability of sharing my desperation with others. Help me today to lay my needs at Your feet, and show me the ongoing miracle of how You provide. Amen.

DAY 3: SIDE BY SIDE

Read God's Word

Today our experience walking through Scripture will look a little different. The story of Jesus feeding five thousand offers us a unique chance to look at four different Gospels telling the same story. This is a unique opportunity because the feeding of the five thousand is the only miracle of Jesus other than the Resurrection told in all four Gospels.

In case you missed the importance of that statement, let me say it in a different way: Of all the stories told of Jesus' miracles, this is the only one that was retold by all four Gospel authors. Joseph Martin says that simple fact is actually a gigantic indicator "that provides a gauge for how dramatic, memorable, and important [this] event was for the disciples and the early church."[3]

So for our study today, I'd like you to spend some time with the four Gospel accounts of this miracle. To begin, read through all four accounts on page 57.

Reflect and Respond

Now that you've read through all four accounts, I'd like to guide you in exploring the different accounts on your own, noticing their similarities and differences, before we look at some insights together. If you enjoy color-coding, grab some highlighters. If you'd like to use symbols such as underlining, circles, stars, boxes, or parentheses and brackets, one pen or pencil will do.

First, take note of the similarities you find between the accounts. Use one color or symbol to mark some of the things listed below, as well as other similarities you notice. You can mark things that occur in all four stories or things that are the same in two or three Gospels. (For example, you might mark the mention of the grass people were sitting on in green highlighter in all four passages.)

- Some of the similarities you might mark include the following:
  o Jesus and the disciples withdrawing to be alone
  o descriptions of the location (shore, grass, deserted place)
  o Jesus' direction to the disciples ("You give them something to eat")
  o Jesus' instructions to the people to sit down
  o the amount of bread and fish found
  o Jesus' actions when He offers the bread (giving thanks, taking, blessing, breaking it)
  o the distribution to the people by the disciples
  o the amount of leftovers

What other similarities did you notice and mark? List them below:

Matthew 14:13-21

[13]When Jesus heard what had happened, he withdrew by boat privately to a solitary place. Hearing of this, the crowds followed him on foot from the towns. [14]When Jesus landed and saw a large crowd, he had compassion on them and healed their sick.

[15]As evening approached, the disciples came to him and said, "This is a remote place, and it's already getting late. Send the crowds away, so they can go to the villages and buy themselves some food."

[16]Jesus replied, "They do not need to go away. You give them something to eat."

[17]"We have here only five loaves of bread and two fish," they answered.

[18]"Bring them here to me," he said. [19]And he directed the people to sit down on the grass. Taking the five loaves and the two fish and looking up to heaven, he gave thanks and broke the loaves. Then he gave them to the disciples, and the disciples gave them to the people. [20]They all ate and were satisfied, and the disciples picked up twelve basketfuls of broken pieces that were left over. [21]The number of those who ate was about five thousand men, besides women and children.

Mark 6:32-44

[32]So they went away by themselves in a boat to a solitary place. [33]But many who saw them leaving recognized them and ran on foot from all the towns and got there ahead of them. [34]When Jesus landed and saw a large crowd, he had compassion on them, because they were like sheep without a shepherd. So he began teaching them many things.

[35]By this time it was late in the day, so his disciples came to him. "This is a remote place," they said, "and it's already very late. [36]Send the people away so that they can go to the surrounding countryside and villages and buy themselves something to eat."

[37]But he answered, "You give them something to eat."

They said to him, "That would take more than half a year's wages! Are we to go and spend that much on bread and give it to them to eat?"

[38]"How many loaves do you have?" he asked. "Go and see."

When they found out, they said, "Five—and two fish."

[39]Then Jesus directed them to have all the people sit down in groups on the green grass. [40]So they sat down in groups of hundreds and fifties. [41]Taking the five loaves and the two fish and looking up to heaven, he gave thanks and broke the loaves. Then he gave them to his disciples to distribute to the people. He also divided the two fish among them all. [42]They all ate and were satisfied, [43]and the disciples picked up twelve basketfuls of broken pieces of bread and fish. [44]The number of the men who had eaten was five thousand.

Luke 9:10-17

[10]When the apostles returned, they reported to Jesus what they had done. Then he took them with him and they withdrew by themselves to a town called Bethsaida, [11]but the crowds learned about it and followed him. He welcomed them and spoke to them about the kingdom of God, and healed those who needed healing.

[12]Late in the afternoon the Twelve came to him and said, "Send the crowd away so they can go to the surrounding villages and countryside and find food and lodging, because we are in a remote place here."

[13]He replied, "You give them something to eat."

They answered, "We have only five loaves of bread and two fish—unless we go and buy food for all this crowd." [14](About five thousand men were there.)

But he said to his disciples, "Have them sit down in groups of about fifty each." [15]The disciples did so, and everyone sat down. [16]Taking the five loaves and the two fish and looking up to heaven, he gave thanks and broke them. Then he gave them to the disciples to distribute to the people. [17]They all ate and were satisfied, and the disciples picked up twelve basketfuls of broken pieces that were left over.

John 6:3-14

[3]Then Jesus went up on a mountainside and sat down with his disciples. [4]The Jewish Passover Festival was near.

[5]When Jesus looked up and saw a great crowd coming toward him, he said to Philip, "Where shall we buy bread for these people to eat?" [6]He asked this only to test him, for he already had in mind what he was going to do.

[7]Philip answered him, "It would take more than half a year's wages to buy enough bread for each one to have a bite!"

[8]Another of his disciples, Andrew, Simon Peter's brother, spoke up, [9]"Here is a boy with five small barley loaves and two small fish, but how far will they go among so many?"

[10]Jesus said, "Have the people sit down." There was plenty of grass in that place, and they sat down (about five thousand men were there). [11]Jesus then took the loaves, gave thanks, and distributed to those who were seated as much as they wanted. He did the same with the fish.

[12]When they had all had enough to eat, he said to his disciples, "Gather the pieces that are left over. Let nothing be wasted." [13]So they gathered them and filled twelve baskets with the pieces of the five barley loaves left over by those who had eaten.

[14]After the people saw the sign Jesus performed, they began to say, "Surely this is the Prophet who is to come into the world."

Note: All Scriptures are NIV.

Next, use a color or symbol to mark the differences you find in the stories.

- Some of the differences you might mark include the following:
    - In Matthew, Jesus compares the people to sheep without a shepherd.
    - In Matthew and Luke, Jesus heals people; in Mark and Luke, Jesus teaches people; but in John we don't hear about either one.
    - In John, we see the presence of the little boy and Andrew's role.
    - In Mark, we hear about people sitting in groups of fifty and one hundred.
    - John adds details such as the time of year (Passover), the type of bread, the fact that Jesus gives thanks over the bread, and the reaction of the crowd after the miracle.
    - In Matthew, the count of people is mentioned at five thousand men (besides women and children).

What other differences do you notice? You might look for differences in tone and delivery. Is one Gospel more concise? One more action driven? One more detailed? Highlight or mark these and any other differences you see.

Which three Gospel accounts are more similar to one another?

Which of the accounts differs the most from the others?

What questions do you have based on some of your observations?

As we continue reading other miracle stories in the coming weeks, we'll see that some miracles are told in more than one Gospel—with many similarities and some differences—while some stories are told in only one or two of the Gospels. The first three Gospels (Matthew, Mark, and Luke) are the most alike and are called *synoptic*, meaning "seeing together," because they can be viewed side by side for comparison.

John is the outlier, since it was written later than the others and with much more of a theological than chronological emphasis. John, for example, wants to highlight that there are seven signs or miracles, because the number seven is significant theologically. He records long discourses of Jesus' teaching and shapes stories and conversations in a lyrical, almost poetic way. Like the other Gospel writers, what John wants us to see shapes how he tells the story.[4]

Now, let's look together quickly at a few aspects of this week's miracle story of the feeding of the five thousand and consider how the very same story can be told differently by different authors speaking to different audiences.

1. The Setting

Each of the Gospel writers gives us details that set the scene for this miracle. Matthew gives us a concise account of Jesus going away to a deserted place and the crowds following Him. Mark gives the same details but adds that Jesus took the disciples along too. Mark is the most detailed and action-packed account, with lots of action verbs thrown in. While Luke sticks with the facts, he tells us that Jesus is in the region of Bethsaida, a name that means "House of Fish,"[5] highlighting the fish that will be part of the meal to come. John includes the element of timing, telling us that this is Passover. This detail makes it even richer when we see them sharing a meal together, as Jews did at Passover to mark the freedom given them in the Exodus. John is always calling our attention to symbols that will be the signs pointing to different aspects of Jesus' ministry, and this sign helps us see the freedom Jesus wants to bring to God's people the way Moses brought freedom to the Israelites.

Mark also is the one who connects for us the setting of green grass (mentioned in more than one account), Jesus' vision of the people as sheep without a shepherd, and the command for people to "recline"—showing a banquet. These details have echoes of Psalm 23: "The Lord is my shepherd.../ He makes me lie down in green pastures." (More about that tomorrow!)

Even the way the various Gospels provide a setting for the story shows us how a different viewpoint can call our attention to different aspects of the message.

2. The Problem

The four accounts also paint for us a picture of the problem, each bringing a different nuance or emphasis just as four persons retelling the same story would do. Matthew again presents the basic facts of the situation: the place is

The authors Matthew and Luke almost certainly read Mark's Gospel and used it as a source, since 91 percent of Mark's information reappears in Matthew or Luke—and often in both. When emphasis differs in the three, it's often because of the different audiences they were writing to (Matthew: Jewish; Mark: Greek; Luke: Roman).

isolated, the hour is late, and the disciples suggest sending the people away. Mark expands on those facts and hints at an emotional urgency in his tone by emphasizing how late it is and the amount of money that would be necessary to buy bread. Luke adds the practical detail of lodging, noting that the people should also look for a place to stay. John shows more individual conversation between the disciples, emphasizing Philip's practicality and then telling how Andrew brought the boy forward with the resources that would provide a solution.

Every Gospel indicates how desperate the situation of encountering a hungry crowd can be, but each one emphasizes a different aspect of the conditions we find there.

3. The Motions or Actions

As different as the accounts are, they suddenly converge and come to almost surprising accuracy in agreement about the details of exactly how Jesus handles the meal in this story.

- Through the disciples, Jesus commands the people to sit.
- Jesus takes the bread.
- Jesus looks up to heaven.
- Jesus blesses/gives thanks.
- Jesus breaks/divides the elements. (John is the only one who doesn't indicate that Jesus breaks the elements.)
- Jesus distributes the elements through the disciples.

This tight consistency in the set of events indicates a desire to tell the story in a way that mirrors closely the Lord's Supper, which we will consider again in our study tomorrow. Although the feeding of the five thousand occurs before the Last Supper, which happens on the night before Jesus' death, we must remember that the authors were writing their Gospels *after* Jesus' death and resurrection. They would have recognized the similarities between the actions on that hillside and the actions in the upper room and wanted people reading to see them as well.

4. The Outcome

All four Gospel accounts proclaim the same outcome—that the whole crowd was filled. This wasn't just the edge being taken off their hunger; they were satisfied! And there was enough for leftovers, filling twelve baskets. In John's Gospel, people react by comparing Jesus to a prophet. All of the accounts also agree that once the crowds were fed, Jesus went on His way up the mountain to be alone; however, only John mentions that the crowd was pursuing and trying to make Him king (John 6:15). It becomes clear that the way the story started, with Jesus longing to have some time alone for prayer and rest, is the way that the story ends—with His wishes being fulfilled.

For some, reading the different accounts of Jesus' life in the four Gospels causes confusion or doubt. They wonder: Why do we have four stories of Jesus' life? How do four different accounts of the same story have four different sets of details? Others have speculated that the stories contradict one another and should cause us to doubt the accuracy of the accounts.

But the differences in the different ways that the Gospel writers tell the stories actually *add* to their credibility, not detract from it. They are doing their job according to their own first-century culture, not according to ours in the twenty-first century.

Many biblical scholars have warned us not to read the Gospels as if they are modern biographies. Our modern biographers are expected to be impartial, detached observers, writing down what we'd call "just the facts"—and as many facts, dates, and details as possible. But in the time the Gospels were written, it was entirely acceptable—and even expected—that the Gospel writers were interpreting the facts as they went, using the *way* they wrote the story to get across the points they wanted us to hear. It was expected that they would change the order of the sequence of events or emphasize or leave out a detail if it meant getting their theological point across to their intended audience.[6]

So, rather than be bothered by the differences you see in different accounts of the miracle stories as we read and study, be a curious observer of the details. As you read, ask God, "How can what I am reading help me grow in relationship to You?" And always remember that whenever you read God's Word, you are holding a treasure in your hands, the very breath of God—for "all Scripture is God-breathed and is useful for teaching, rebuking, correcting and training in righteousness, so that the servant of God may be thoroughly equipped for every good work" (2 Timothy 3:16-17 NIV).

Talk with God

Lord, as I read Your Word, help it sink into every part of who I am. Let it inform and form my working, playing, thinking, and being. Thank You for the precious treasure You have placed in my hands. Help me always to hold it—and myself—in a way so that others will see You in me. Amen.

DAY 4: ECHOES OF ABUNDANCE

Read God's Word

[8]*Then the word of the* LORD *came to [Elijah]:* [9]*"Go at once to Zarephath in the region of Sidon and stay there. I have directed a widow there to supply you with food."* [10]*So*

he went to Zarephath. When he came to the town gate, a widow was there gathering sticks. He called to her and asked, "Would you bring me a little water in a jar so I may have a drink?" ¹¹As she was going to get it, he called, "And bring me, please, a piece of bread."

¹²"As surely as the Lord your God lives," she replied, "I don't have any bread—only a handful of flour in a jar and a little olive oil in a jug. I am gathering a few sticks to take home and make a meal for myself and my son, that we may eat it—and die."

¹³Elijah said to her, "Don't be afraid. Go home and do as you have said. But first make a small loaf of bread for me from what you have and bring it to me, and then make something for yourself and your son. ¹⁴For this is what the Lord, the God of Israel, says: 'The jar of flour will not be used up and the jug of oil will not run dry until the day the Lord sends rain on the land.'"

¹⁵She went away and did as Elijah had told her. So there was food every day for Elijah and for the woman and her family. ¹⁶For the jar of flour was not used up and the jug of oil did not run dry, in keeping with the word of the Lord spoken by Elijah.

(1 Kings 17:8-16 NIV)

Reflect and Respond

We use stories to tell stories all the time. If you're hearing a tale described as "a real Cinderella story," you immediately know that it's about someone rising from a low position to shine in prominence. A tax described as a "Robin Hood" tax makes you think of a story where someone takes from the rich to give to the poor. Describe someone as a "Scrooge," a "Don Juan," or a bit of a "Jekyll and Hyde" (or even a "Judas"), and you're using a literary allusion to a story to explain what you mean about the story you are telling.

Stories are often used to illuminate stories. When people experienced or heard the story of Jesus feeding the multitude, what other events did it bring to mind? There are allusions scattered throughout the story of Jesus feeding thousands on the hillside that immediately would have brought other events to mind for the hearers, and those echoes would have given them some clue about God and His larger story—clues that we might miss unless we delve into the background of some of these events.

What can we learn about the story of the feeding of the five thousand if we examine the stories hidden within the story? The Gospel writers wanted this story to feel very familiar, bringing up the memories of how faithful God had been to them in past situations. This story highlights that God's saving acts through miraculous means have been going on for a long time. It tells us that God is faithful and can be trusted. Today as we dig under the surface of this miracle account, we will unearth some wonderful references to God's abundant

provision, power, compassion, and faithfulness throughout Scripture. So, let's look together at some of these stories within the story that speak of God's abundance.

Moses

One story within this miracle story of the feeding of the five thousand has to do with Moses leading God's people to freedom through the wilderness. As we learned yesterday, John seems to give a random detail in his Gospel account of this miracle without elaboration or explanation, noting that it was near the time of the Passover (John 6:4). Though we briefly considered this detail earlier in the week, let's take another look.

Each year during the Passover Feast, God's people remembered and rehearsed the story of God's faithfulness in their escape from slavery in Egypt. During the meal, they remembered the wilderness wanderings and the miraculous ways God abundantly provided for His hungry and thirsty people by bringing the miracles of water, quail, and manna—a bread provided from heaven new every morning (see Exodus 16). The crowd of hungry people who are abundantly fed by Jesus soon will be celebrating the Passover, which commemorates God's abundant provision.

The very next day a crowd hears about the miraculous feeding, goes to find Jesus, and engages in conversation with Him, wondering if He's a kind of new Moses because He has brought them bread. This intriguing conversation, which begins in John 6:25, culminates with Jesus making an astounding promise: "I am the bread of life. Whoever comes to me will never be hungry, and whoever believes in me will never be thirsty" (John 6:35).

Instead of just another prophet bringing bread that will be eaten up, Jesus proclaims that He Himself *is* the bread of life! This statement simultaneously points back to the Exodus—indicating God is about to free His people from slavery—and points forward to the Last Supper and the cross.

When times are difficult or dry in your own life, what are some miraculous moments of God's presence or provision that you can look back on to draw strength?

Elijah

The feeding of the five thousand also echoes one of the greatest stories of abundance found in Scripture: the encounter of the prophet Elijah and the widow of Zarephath, which you read at the beginning of today's lesson. This woman was at such a point of desperation that when she met the prophet, she was in the process of gathering a few sticks to cook what she thought was her last meal. Even more heartbreaking, she had a son, whom she thought would die of starvation along with herself.

Elijah comforted her by telling her not to be afraid, promising that God would take care of her and her son until the severe drought of her country ended; but first he asked her to do something unheard of.

Reread 1 Kings 17:13. What did Elijah ask her to do?

Can you imagine! She has only enough for one last meal, and a complete stranger is asking that she make him a loaf of bread first!

In an act of faith that we may not be able to comprehend, the widow faithfully follows his instruction. What a beautiful parallel to the faith of the little boy in the crowd who, instead of hoarding his resources, offers them to Jesus and sees them multiply beyond his wildest dreams.

I love the picture of abundance that follows in Elijah's story.

Reread 1 Kings 17:16. What happened next?

Each time she dipped into the flour, there was enough. Each time she poured oil out of the jug, there was enough, and this happened again and again until the drought and famine passed. This must have taken a daily act of faith on her part—first to give her "last loaf" to the prophet, and then to go to her pantry day after day and find that God provided, literally, her daily bread.

Can you think of a time God provided for your needs (physically, spiritually, or emotionally) just when you thought you had run out? If so, describe it below:

Elisha

Another story of abundance within this miracle story has to do with the prophet Elisha. The stories of the prophet Elijah and his protégé, the younger prophet Elisha, are a favorite topic of mine. In my study *Set Apart: Holy Habits of Prophets and Kings*, I talk about how Elisha asked God for a double portion of the spirit of his mentor Elijah once the elder man was gone. Indeed, if you follow Elisha's ministry, many of his miracles are echoes of Elijah's earlier miracles, and (depending on how you count) he did perform double the number of miracles of Elijah.

Elijah's encounter with the widow of Zarephath, when God multiplied the flour and oil for her and her son, is echoed in a later miracle that Elisha performed. Yet another widow is in a desperate situation where her creditors are about to take her sons as slaves if she cannot pay her debts (2 Kings 4:1-7). Elisha asks her, "What do you have in your house?" (4:2 NIV), and she mentions a small jar of olive oil. He instructs her to borrow all the empty bottles and jars she can from her neighbors and begin pouring the small jar of oil into each of them. When she does, she finds it keeps pouring and pouring! Finally, when the last borrowed jar is filled, the oil stops. She sells the oil and pays her debts, and once again God has multiplied another tiny resource into a big solution.

But it is yet another of Elisha's miracles that bears even closer resemblance to Jesus' miracle of feeding five thousand.

Read 2 Kings 4:42-44. How many loaves are there?

How many men do they feed? (Notice there are leftovers, just as in the story of Jesus feeding the multitude!)

There's one more detail of this story I don't want you to miss.

Read 2 Kings 4:42 and John 6:9, 13 in the margin. What kind of bread is used in each story?

> *A man came from Baal-shalishah, bringing food from the first fruits to the man of God: twenty loaves of barley and fresh ears of grain in his sack. Elisha said, "Give it to the people and let them eat."*
> *(2 Kings 4:42)*

> [9]*"There is a boy here who has five barley loaves and two fish. But what are they among so many people?"…*[13]*So they gathered them up, and from the fragments of the five barley loaves, left by those who had eaten, they filled twelve baskets.*
> *(John 6:9, 13)*

Barley loaves, which were small, rustic loaves of bread, were the food of the poor. Any of God's people listening to this story and hearing about the barley loaves would immediately think of Elisha's story and be amazed by the greater numbers that Jesus fed. The main echo would be the abundance of God that resounds throughout Scripture.

Psalm 23

As we consider the stories within this story of the feeding of five thousand, we must make mention of Psalm 23. Perhaps one of the best-known passages in

Scripture, this psalm paints a pastoral scene of a good shepherd caring for his sheep—an allusion to the overflowing kindness of Jesus, the Good Shepherd, taking care of His sheep. As we noted briefly yesterday, many details of the story of the feeding of five thousand echo the shepherd story. Let's look at a few of them.

Extra Insight

Jesus has the people "sit down" (John 6:10). The Greek word *anepeson* translated here as "sit down" literally means to recline. Reclining is the posture for a banquet.[7]

Answer the questions in the column on the right to complete the chart:

Psalm 23	Feeding of Five Thousand
"The LORD is my shepherd" (23:1)	How does Jesus describe the crowds in Mark 6:34?
"He makes me lie down in green pastures" (23:2) Abundant food and soft surroundings	What description of the setting do we find in John 6:10 (also see Matthew 4:19 and Mark 6:39)?
"He leads me beside quiet waters" (23:2 NIV) Abundant drink and beautiful scenery	What is the location of the miracle according to John 6:1-3?
"You prepare a table before me" (23:5) Echoes the many descriptions of the banquet of the kingdom of God in the Old Testament	In John 6:10, what does Jesus have the people do? (See Extra Insight for deeper understanding.)

The Last Supper

The last story within a story found in the feeding of five thousand is not an echo backward in time but a foreshadowing of what is to come at the Last Supper in the upper room. Though we touched on this yesterday, let's take time to compare the texts and consider the implications of their similarities.

Read the Scriptures we see below, and list the actions we see in each:

Actions in Matthew 14:19   **Actions in Matthew 26:26-28**

The acts of taking the loaves, blessing them, breaking them, and giving them to His disciples echo Jesus' actions at the Last Supper as He offers the bread and cup to His disciples. Don't miss the significance of the similarities. These parallels let us know that the miracle of miraculous multiplication didn't end on that day on the hillside. We are included *every* time we participate in the blessing, breaking, and offering of bread and wine. Jesus is the bread of life, and He came to satisfy the deep needs of the world—the deep needs of you and of me. The abundance of that day is evidence of God's desire to abundantly provide for our needs today.

As we've reflected on these stories within the story—connecting the dots and putting them together—I hope you've recognized that God's abundance is greater than you ever imagined. I'm reminded of Paul's words to the Philippians, which are still true today for each one of us: "And my God will meet all your needs according to the riches of his glory in Christ Jesus" (Philippians 4:19 NIV).

End your study today by reflecting on the ways God has met your needs in moments of desperation with His unlimited abundance, and in the margin, write a prayer of thanks to God for His glorious riches.

Talk with God

Jesus, I am grateful that You are the same yesterday, today, and forever. As I examine the places in my life right now where I see famine and those where I see abundance, remind me of Your ability to always give me more than enough. Amen.

DAY 5: AN ABUNDANT CATCH

Read God's Word

[1]One day as Jesus was standing by the Lake of Gennesaret, the people were crowding around him and listening to the word of God. [2]He saw at the water's edge two boats, left there by the fishermen, who were washing their nets. [3]He got into one of the boats,

the one belonging to Simon, and asked him to put out a little from shore. Then he sat down and taught the people from the boat.

[4]When he had finished speaking, he said to Simon, "Put out into deep water, and let down the nets for a catch."

[5]Simon answered, "Master, we've worked hard all night and haven't caught anything. But because you say so, I will let down the nets."

[6]When they had done so, they caught such a large number of fish that their nets began to break. [7]So they signaled their partners in the other boat to come and help them, and they came and filled both boats so full that they began to sink.

[8]When Simon Peter saw this, he fell at Jesus' knees and said, "Go away from me, Lord; I am a sinful man!" [9]For he and all his companions were astonished at the catch of fish they had taken, [10]and so were James and John, the sons of Zebedee, Simon's partners.

Then Jesus said to Simon, "Don't be afraid; from now on you will fish for people." [11]So they pulled their boats up on shore, left everything and followed him.

(Luke 5:1-11 NIV)

Reflect and Respond

Remember making wish lists as a kid? When it came time for Christmas or your birthday, did you write a list of everything you could possibly want? Or did you circle items and dog-ear pages in a catalog? I remember going through the many catalogs we would get in the mail (my mom was a teacher so we got some great ones!), circling items and leaving subtle notes like "I really want this!" and then leaving them carefully placed on the coffee table and hoping my mom would get the hint.

What were some of the things you remember wishing for as a child?

What would be on your grown-up wish list? Write your list below:

Now, imagine getting *every single thing* on that list—a haul so big that your arms couldn't even carry it! What would your response be?

The disciple Simon Peter experienced a fulfillment of his wish list that meant success beyond his dreams, but his response may be surprising.

Let me set the scene. We're at the beginning of Jesus' ministry. According to the ordering of events in Luke's Gospel, here is what has happened so far:

- Jesus is baptized by John the Baptist (Luke 3).
- Jesus is tempted by Satan during his forty-day fast in the wilderness (Luke 4).
- Jesus preaches a sermon that gets Him thrown out of His hometown synagogue in Nazareth (Luke 4).
- Jesus travels to the towns surrounding the Sea of Galilee and begins doing things that astonish people: He casts an evil spirit out of a man and goes to Simon Peter's house where He heals Peter's mother-in-law of a fever (Luke 4).
- Now people are bringing those who are sick and demon possessed to Jesus, and He is healing them (Luke 4).

Crowds of people are starting to gather. They love listening to Jesus and are amazed at His teaching, because He speaks with authority (Luke 4:32), as well as the power and authority with which He commands demons and heals people. The more public miracles that Jesus performs, the more the crowds come.

He's teaching the crowds on the shore of Galilee one day, and they're crowding him to the very edge. Jesus looks out and sees two boats and an opportunity. He calls them over and uses one of the boats as a floating pulpit to teach the crowds, an ingenious solution to being able to be near enough to teach but not so close that the crowds push against Him while He does it. Then He turns to Peter, the owner of the particular boat He's in, and gives an unusual order.

Reread Luke 5:4. What does Jesus tell Peter to do?

This order is directed straight at Peter. Even though there are other fishermen present, this story is told with a spotlight on Peter, because it's a one-to-one conversation. Of all those in the boats, only Peter speaks to Jesus. And when Jesus speaks, He addresses only Peter, using singular verbs: "Don't be afraid; from now on you will fish for people" (Luke 5:10 NIV).

Consider what's going through Peter's mind. He's tired and skeptical. It's dubious that this carpenter from a neighboring town can just jump in a boat and seem to know Peter's trade better than he does. It's clear that they've been out all night (a typical time for fishing), have tried every trick they know as professionals, and have come up empty. It would be easy for Peter to refuse. Jesus has already asked the favor of using the boat to teach from; wasn't that enough? But two things push Peter to trust Jesus enough to give it a try: 1) Peter's desperation and (2) Jesus' reputation. Let's consider each.

1. *Peter's desperation*. Peter has tried everything and has come up empty. Why not give Jesus a try? This is often true in our lives as well. We try everything we can in our own strength, and we only find failure; so Jesus is a last resort. The good news is that Jesus doesn't reject us just because we take a while to do it His way.

Have you ever had a time when you tried everything and came up empty? If so, reflect on that season below:

2. *Jesus' reputation*. Don't forget that Jesus has just healed Peter's mother-in-law in Peter's own house (Luke 4:38-39). Peter has witnessed Jesus' healing work firsthand. He's seen the crowds gather in awe of Jesus' miraculous actions. And he's just had a front-row seat to Jesus' amazing teaching preached from his own boat!

How would you describe Jesus' reputation at this point in His ministry based on what we've considered from Luke's Gospel?

When these two things come together—feeling desperate after our failure to do it alone and witnessing or hearing about the power of Jesus—there's a good chance we'll turn to Him, which is what Peter did.

Reread Luke 5:5. What reason does Peter give for letting down the nets?

Can you hear the ho-hum tone in Peter's response? "Okay, Lord, if you say so…" Yet despite his lack of enthusiasm, he receives an incredible, overflowing answer.

Reread Luke 5:6-7. What do we learn about the catch?

The nets are so full of fish that they are in danger of breaking! So the other boat comes over to help, and then even the boats are in danger of sinking!

Most of us have been like Peter at one time or another, saying unenthusiastically, "OK, Lord, if you say so…"

When has the Lord given you some instructions that you obeyed hesitantly or doubtfully?

What happened?

To say Peter and his companions are astonished at the abundance of fish is an understatement. This is a catch like never before, a success beyond their wildest dreams. Later those in the boat would witness Jesus calming a storm and say, "Who is this? Even the wind and the waves obey him!" (Mark 4:41 NIV). In this moment, I can imagine them asking one another, "Who is this? Even the *fish* obey him!" This is like Christmas morning, a free cruise, and an unexpected windfall of money all rolled into one.

But once Peter calms down a bit, he realizes something. He begins to sense that this moment is about more than just fish—that Jesus is about to call him to do something more, to be something more. So he sinks to his knees in front of Jesus and begs Him to leave.

What does Peter say to Jesus in Luke 5:8?

Peter tells Jesus to "go away from me" not just because of his past but also because of what may come next. He's not the only one, of course, to resist a calling from God. Most persons in the Bible who are called by God begin by resisting their calling. Moses, Isaiah, Esther, and Jeremiah all tried to find loopholes to get out of their callings. Peter's insistence that he is sinful and inadequate to follow and serve follows a pattern of others in Scripture who have found the presence of God's holiness to be a spotlight on their own unholiness.

Read the Scriptures below to find others in Scripture who felt unworthy of God's calling for them. Who were they and how did God answer their fears and doubts?

	Person	God's Answer
Exodus 3:11-12		
Judges 6:15-16		
Isaiah 6:5-8		

Have _you_ ever felt inadequate or unworthy to answer God's call? If so, describe it and tell how God responded to your fears and doubts.

> **It's common for us to feel unworthy in the presence of the divine, but God always answers with the assurance that it is not our worthiness that counts.**

It's common for us to feel unworthy in the presence of the divine, but God always answers with the assurance that it is not our worthiness that counts. God's power and holiness are what cleanse us when we're called to serve, and then He powers our ministry.

This week we've been exploring abundance and examining those times and places when God produced much where there was little or none in people's lives. It's a common temptation for us to see Jesus' miracles as an answer to our wish lists—just as it is a common anguish for us to wonder what we've done wrong if our dearest wishes haven't been fulfilled even after we have been faithful to God. As Peter witnesses this miracle of the abundant catch, he seems to be experiencing a dream come true and an undoing almost simultaneously.

Mark Buchanan imagines what is going through Peter's mind at this moment: the inner conflict between focusing on the abundance of wealth in the nets and focusing on the calling to follow Jesus. If Jesus' role is to fulfill our wishes, then He is there to serve Peter. But Jesus has something else in mind: for Peter to leave it all behind to serve Jesus. Buchanan writes:

> Jesus' calling is not to follow Peter. His role and task in life is not to advance Peter's career, enhance Peter's reputation, thicken Peter's wallet. Peter sees all that in Jesus' eyes. He sees that Jesus is not the man who exists simply to come onto our fish boats and fill up our nets. Peter must know what Jesus is about to say: "Follow me." Which means—ah, why does it have to mean this?—*leave everything*. The fish. The boat. The nets. The safety. The security. The prospects.
>
> Leave everything.
>
> Now imagine the moment. Peter falls on his face, begs Jesus to leave. Depart from me.
>
> Somebody's got to leave. Either Peter leaves everything, or Jesus leaves Peter.
>
> That happens every day somewhere. Jesus comes onto our boat and fills up our nets—a job promotion, a new house, a new car, a big raise. And our prayer is: "Oh, Lord, depart from me." Which means: "Don't take it away. You leave me alone, Jesus, so that I don't have to leave this behind. Go away and don't interfere with my unbridled pleasure-taking in it.
>
> But I'll call if the fishing gets scarce again.[8]

We have to remember what happens at the very end of this story. The fishermen leave everything: the full nets, the boats, their careers, their families, and their homes. Everything they've ever had on a wish list is nothing compared to following Jesus. When God brings abundance into our lives, it's not the gift that deserves our attention, it's the Giver. All of the abundance miracles are simply indicators of the abundant God behind it all—the One who desires our service, our worship, and our all.

Peter is a great example of abundance turning our hearts not to the gift, but to the Giver. When he first addresses Jesus in this story, he calls Jesus "Master," the Greek name used to address tutors or teachers. But after he pulls up the fish, he addresses him as "Lord."[9]

Have you professed that Jesus is Lord over everything you have and everything you are today? Think about all the wishes and prayers you've seen become reality in your life—all the abundance that is before you. Now turn to the God in your boat—His eyes sparkling as He looks over the nets and

When God brings abundance into our lives, it's not the gift that deserves our attention, it's the Giver.

calls your gaze up from the catch to Himself, saying: "Follow me." How will you respond?

Talk with God

Lord, You are the Giver, the miracle-worker, the One who gives me more than I could ask or imagine. Help me to trust You when I've tried on my own and come up empty. Bring to my mind this story of an overflowing net of fish and the call to follow You. Take my whole life—all of it: my dreams, my talents, my family, and even my ideas about what I'm supposed to do. You are the Lord over all of it. I will follow. Amen.

VIDEO VIEWER GUIDE: WEEK 2

Where our _____ runs out is where Jesus' _____ begins. *

"I am the bread of life. Whoever comes to me will never be hungry, and whoever believes in me will never be thirsty."—John 6:35

"Those who eat my flesh and drink my blood abide in me, and I in them."—John 6:56

Jesus feeds us with _____.

Jesus, the _____ of _____, never runs out.

Bread   Life

Week 3

MIRACLES ON THE WATER

Even the Wind and Waves Obey Him

DAY 1: PEACE! BE STILL

Read God's Word

³⁵On that day, when evening had come, he said to them, "Let us go across to the other side." ³⁶And leaving the crowd behind, they took him with them in the boat, just as he was. Other boats were with him. ³⁷A great windstorm arose, and the waves beat into the boat, so that the boat was already being swamped. ³⁸But he was in the stern, asleep on the cushion; and they woke him up and said to him, "Teacher, do you not care that we are perishing?"

³⁹He woke up and rebuked the wind, and said to the sea, "Peace! Be still!" Then the wind ceased, and there was a dead calm.

⁴⁰He said to them, "Why are you afraid? Have you still no faith?"

⁴¹And they were filled with great awe and said to one another, "Who then is this, that even the wind and the sea obey him?"

(Mark 4:35-41)

Reflect and Respond

From an early age, I was fascinated with the Impressionist painters. Rembrandt is one of my favorites. While I've always admired the glorious colors and tranquil expressions of his portraits and still lifes, the one painting that captivates me most is full of both motion and emotion, *Christ in the Storm on the Sea of Galilee.*

This is the only seascape that Rembrandt ever painted, and it's a tumultuous moment frozen in time. A small boat packed with disciples tilts precariously, almost capsized in the middle of a raging storm. Light and dark (Rembrandt's specialty) show us white-capped waves and dark clouds. The scene looks bleak, but if you look closely you can spot a hopeful patch of blue sky peeking through the storm, an indication of what's to come.

Take a moment now to do an Internet image search using the title of the painting *Christ in the Storm* and Rembrandt's name. How would you describe the expressions and actions of the disciples in the boat?

Now do a head count. How many disciples are in the boat? (Look carefully since some are tucked away in the shadows.)

If you zoom in and search the anxious faces in the boat, you'll find them in all kinds of positions and postures: some are fighting the sails or straining at the oars, another is seemingly seasick over the side, one is praying, and some are turning toward Jesus. In the center of it all, a tranquil Jesus sleeps, resting just as peacefully as if safe on dry land. And when you do a head count, you'll find thirteen disciples in addition to Jesus at the center of the scene. Thirteen! If that number seems off to you, you're not alone.

The disciple smack in the middle of the painting is the only one seeming to make eye contact directly with us. His young face distressed, he's hanging onto his hat even as he hangs onto a rope that keeps him from falling overboard. This young man's face at the center of the action looks remarkably like self-portraits that Rembrandt painted of himself—and for good reason. Rembrandt painted himself into the center of his picture! It seems he got so personally invested in this biblical story that he literally put himself inside the scene he depicted on canvas.

In his painting, Rembrandt is right in the middle of the action. In your life, when have you found yourself in the middle of a storm? Circle the words from our scene that seem similar to your reactions to your own storm:

Fighting	**Praying**	**Worrying God has forgotten you**
Turning to Jesus	**Feeling sick keep going**	**Straining to**

List other responses here:

Of all Jesus' miracles, this is probably the one most of us can identify with. We've all experienced storms of chaos, anxiety, struggles, and worry. When life presents conditions that are chaotic and out of our control, we might take any of the postures found in the Rembrandt painting: bewildered, sick, fighting, praying, reaching out to Jesus. (Sometimes we even go through all of them!) Finding out what happened in the moment of the real-life storm may give us some insight into how Jesus is present with us in the storms we're presented with on dry land.

The miracles we're looking at this week all happened on the water. Of all the miracles in the Gospels, these are the only miracles that Jesus performed just for the disciples. Of course, they were present for all of the miracles before this one as bystanders and sometimes beneficiaries. They got to eat some of the bread and fish and drink some of the wine. They watched in awe as people were healed, restored, and resurrected. But the venue for these particular miracles is much more private. The lake where Jesus first met many of the disciples becomes one of the last private places for Him to address their needs, their fears, their desperation. There are no crowds here. No wedding party. No bystanders along dusty streets. These miracles are personal because they address the disciples' desperate moments.

The region around Galilee was home for most of the disciples, and the lake at its center was known for its sudden and violent storms. Cool air masses from the surrounding mountains and fierce winds from the Golan Heights to the east often meet over the warm air of the lake, with resulting storms that crop up so suddenly they can catch even the most experienced sailors off guard.[1] Storms over Galilee were common.

Reread Mark 4:37. What does this description tell us about this particular storm?

This storm must have been a doozy! The wind was high, the waves rough, and the amount of water coming in was already threatening to swamp the boat. The reaction of the disciples said it all: they were terrified. Considering how many of them were professional fishermen, they would not have been disturbed by an insignificant squall. This was a major storm. They honestly believed they were about to die!

While not all of us have been on a small boat in a life-threatening storm, we can all understand the fear and anxiety the disciples experienced. It's easy, like Rembrandt, to put ourselves "in the boat." We can also identify with the immediate and strong reaction of the disciples toward Jesus when their circumstances turned rough.

Take another look at Mark 4:38. What does the disciples' question reveal about their reaction?

The disciples wondered if Jesus even cared. We can relate, can't we? When we are in the midst of extremely hard times, it's so easy to question whether God cares. These disciples had witnessed Jesus going out of His way to heal and help and save so many people from danger and distress. Now it seemed to them that He was sleeping through their hour of greatest need. The good news

God hears our cries over the rumble of the storm, and He knows our heart and our true need.

is that this was no surprise at all to Jesus. He knows our panic, our desperation, our distress. God hears our cries over the rumble of the storm, and He knows our heart and our true need.

Jesus didn't waste any time responding to the disciples' concern.

Reread Mark 4:39. How did Jesus respond to the disciples? What did He do?

Jesus woke and jumped to action to take care of the immediate need of the disciples.

It's significant that the story of the storm is right in the middle of a part of Mark's Gospel highlighting God's kingdom and rule and the truth that because of God's reign, Jesus possesses the power needed to overcome evil and chaos. The section opens in chapter 4 with Jesus telling story after story (parables) explaining God's kingdom and rule (Mark 4:1-34). Then the story we're walking through today shows Jesus using that power to overcome the threatening chaos of the sea. And in chapter 5, when He reaches the other side, Jesus uses this power to do equally amazing things.

Read the following verses in Mark 5, and describe how Jesus uses His power in each situation:

verses 1-20

verses 22-24a

verses 24b-34

verses 35-43

The storm in the middle of the lake is the centerpiece to God's actions of teaching about His power to the crowds on one side and enacting it for the crowds on the other. And here in the middle the disciples get a firsthand demonstration! God's power and compassion for His people are highlighted throughout this section.

Notice that Jesus does not enjoy or encourage storms in our lives. He is not seen as the author of the storm in this story but the One who puts it in its place.

Look again at Mark 4:39. What word is used to describe how Jesus calmed the wind?

What did He say to the sea?

We see that Jesus "rebuked" the wind and the storm—the same word given for His actions of rebuke against the evil spirit He encountered on the other side of the lake (5:1-20). And He spoke peace to the sea. The movement of the power of God is not toward chaos and fear but toward peace.

Just as Jesus' words had immediate effect on the storm, they also had a powerful effect on the disciples. Notice that immediately after Jesus spoke to the storm He spoke to the disciples. He responded in love for these dear friends, who had just been shaking Him and accusing Him of indifference.

Those words, "Be still," should have a familiar ring to them.

Write Psalm 46:10 below:

These words, while they feel like a comfort, are actually a command. Being still in the presence of God even when surrounded by difficult circumstances is not something that comes easily to us. If it did, God would not have had to command us to do it. It's a discipline of obedience and trust, not just a natural gift some people have. When things are difficult, God commands us to be still and turn our eyes to Him.

Think again about the personal storm you recalled earlier. Were you able to turn your eyes to Jesus? What happened?

Reread Mark 4:41. How did the disciples respond to Jesus' power?

The disciples turned their eyes to Jesus and His power, and their attention and emotion changed from fear of the storm to awe of the Savior. The "great

> **When things are difficult, God commands us to be still and turn our eyes to Him.**

> We don't get to choose whether the sea we travel is calm or stormy, but we do get to choose where to turn our eyes and attention. We can choose to be overwhelmed by the power of the storms or overwhelmed by the power of God.

awe" described in this verse could be translated literally: "They feared a great fear."[2] They began the scene in awe of the power the storm might have over their lives, and in the end they were in awe of the kind of power Jesus had over the storm—and thus in their own lives as well.

We don't get to choose whether the sea we travel is calm or stormy, but we do get to choose where to turn our eyes and attention. We can choose to be overwhelmed by the power of the storms or overwhelmed by the power of God. Here's a quick look at the results of those choices:

When we are overcome by the waves:	When we are overcome by awe of God:
We take our cues from the chaos of the storm.	We take our cues from the non-anxious, peaceful heart of the Savior in the storm.
We accuse Jesus of not caring about our storm.	We see that Jesus is in the same boat.
We tell our Savior how big our storm is.	We tell our storm how big our Savior is.

When we feel anxiety or fear at the chaos that every person encounters, we realize just how small and vulnerable we really are. There's a kind of fear that just perpetuates more fear, leading us into the circular thinking that more and more things could go wrong. But then there's a kind of fear that turns our attention to the awe of our Creator.

I hope painting yourself into the center of the storm with Jesus to see what He and the disciples experienced reminds you that while you are small and vulnerable, it is turning your attention to the awesome power of God, not the power of the storm, that brings the greatest awe and comfort. This powerful God cares for you. He has chosen to be in the same boat with you, even in the same storm with you. He is near enough to hear you, know you, and love you up close.

Talk with God

Lord, when storms rise up and create chaos and anxiety in my life, help me to cry out to You. Help me to remember that You're not far off or disinterested but right here in the boat with me. Thank You that You are powerful enough to still any storm that would cause me harm yet gentle enough to still the storms within me. Amen.

DAY 2: JESUS WALKS ON WATER

Read God's Word

^{45}Immediately he made his disciples get into the boat and go on ahead to the other side, to Bethsaida, while he dismissed the crowd. ^{46}After saying farewell to them, he went up on the mountain to pray.

^{47}When evening came, the boat was out on the sea, and he was alone on the land. ^{48}When he saw that they were straining at the oars against an adverse wind, he came towards them early in the morning, walking on the sea. He intended to pass them by. ^{49}But when they saw him walking on the sea, they thought it was a ghost and cried out; ^{50}for they all saw him and were terrified. But immediately he spoke to them and said, "Take heart, it is I; do not be afraid." ^{51}Then he got into the boat with them and the wind ceased. And they were utterly astounded, ^{52}for they did not understand about the loaves, but their hearts were hardened.

(Mark 6:45-52)

Reflect and Respond

Some of the miracles in the Gospels make a lot of sense to me right off the bat. For example, why would Jesus heal a leper, a blind man, and a woman who was bleeding and outcast? Compassion or empathy, a sign of God's goal to move all of creation toward healing and wholeness. What does it reveal about God when Jesus feeds a crowd of hungry people? It is a picture of God's generosity, abundance, and the coming Kingdom where there will be no hunger or thirst. Why does Jesus raise people from the dead? Not only to heal and restore but also to show that He is Lord even over death, a foretaste of what will come in His own resurrection and ours as well.

But here's one that puzzled me at first: Why would Jesus walk on water? What character trait does that display? Whom does it help? Is anyone's life changed in this epic moment—a story so often told we don't usually bother to stop and ask why it happened?

Is this water walk a party trick? Is it: "Hey, guys, watch this!"? That doesn't seem in character for Jesus. His actions are always purposeful, always reflect the character of God, and always move the kingdom of God closer to being a reality on earth as it is in heaven.

So, what is the message behind Jesus walking on water? I'd like to suggest three things: (1) Evil is real. (2) God, who triumphs over evil, is with us. (3) Do not be afraid. Let's examine each message together.

1. Evil Is Real

The miracles and ministry of Jesus are not like a beautiful picture painted on a blank canvas, as if the world is a neutral place in which Jesus proves the power of goodness is the only option. The world is overrun with brokenness and sin, demonstrating that another power besides God is at work. This power is opposite to God's desire for goodness and wholeness but not equal to God's power. Evil is real and is at work in the world.

Each of Jesus' miracles in some way combats the evil powers of the world and shows that God is triumphant over them. The natural world, with its brokenness of sickness, hunger, and death, is a world that Jesus acts to restore and remedy again and again. The spiritual realm—in which sins need forgiveness, relationships need restoration, and souls inhabited by evil spirits need deliverance—is also under God's power and rule.

So, how is evil vanquished by walking on water and calming storms?

In the first-century worldview, the sea symbolized the dwelling place of evil. Think about it. The sea was unpredictable and tumultuous, often stirred with angry and life-threatening storms. Just as we often point upward when we think of heaven, in these ancient times the sea was seen as "the seat of evil on earth."[3]

We find this understanding of the sea from the beginning of the Bible to the end.

The earth was a formless void and darkness covered the face of the deep, while a wind from God swept over the face of the waters.

(Genesis 1:2)

Read Genesis 1:2 in the margin. What covered the "face of the deep," the sea?

Where is God in relation to the waters?

The very beginning of Genesis shows the Spirit of God hovering over the waters. There is darkness, void, and emptiness, but God's Spirit is "over it" and prevails by creating order, light, and fullness. This is also why Revelation depicts the victory of God over evil by describing a sea of glass (Revelation 4:6), meaning that the sea is calm, devoid of any chaos or disorder. In fact, the hymn "Holy, Holy, Holy" refers to Revelation 4:6-11 when it says the elders are "casting down their golden crowns around the glassy sea."[4]

Revelation 15 is even more specific about the relationship of the victorious to the sea of glass.

Read Revelation 15:2 in the margin. Where do the victorious ones stand?

I saw before me what seemed to be a glass sea mixed with fire. And on it stood all the people who had been victorious over the beast and his statue and the number representing his name.
(Revelation 15:2 NLT)

The victorious ones stand *on* the glassy, calm sea! They have conquered and now have no fear. In God's fully redeemed world, their feet actually stand upon the sea, and they have no fear of being swallowed up by the evil that previously made its home there. Even what they considered to be the home of evil is now under God's rule and God's peaceful shalom. When Jesus walks out over the sea, it gives the same kind of picture to the disciples.

How would you explain the "picture" or message that Jesus is giving the disciples when He walks on the water?

Did you note that Jesus is conquering the very place the disciples have feared—the sea? By walking on water He is treading on evil, crushing it under his feet.

This also is true in the story of Jesus calming the storm, which we explored yesterday. When Jesus raised His voice to the evil realm that was threatening to sink the ship, silencing it with the words "Peace! Be still!" (Mark 4:39), He was showing that He has authority not only over the natural world but also over evil itself.

How might recalling Jesus' power and authority help bring calm to a storm in your own life?

2. God, Who Triumphs over Evil, Is with Us

I have always enjoyed the fact that in many stories in the Gospels, the disciples are more than a little clueless. They don't understand Jesus' teaching in the parables, often try to send away the people Jesus wants to care for, and really don't understand the purpose of many of Jesus' miracles. In truth, neither do we! The disciples serve as a stand-in for us in these stories, showing us just how oblivious we often are to the purposes and power of God.

While the disciples were ready for a hero, a new political leader, even a Messiah, they weren't always clear on the fact that Jesus was actually God in human flesh. Jesus would need to reveal that to them as they journeyed together over the years of ministry He spent with them.

Extra Insight

Although Jesus' miracles pointed to the divine power working through Him, that could have been explained as Jesus acting with a power that God gave Him, just as Moses, Elijah, and Elisha worked miracles in the Old Testament. The water miracles in particular, however, show Jesus' divinity, revealing that Jesus is no messenger or middleman; He is God in person.

Today's text gives us a clue that Jesus' miracle of walking on water was intended to reveal to the disciples that He was God in the flesh.

Reread Mark 6:48. What do think Mark means by "pass them by"?

This verse seems strange when we first read it, especially because Jesus did not pass them by but got into the boat. We can gain some understanding from the Old Testament. When Moses asked to see God's glory, God put Moses in the cleft of a rock and covered him until he had passed him by, since seeing God's face would have been too much for Moses to bear (Exodus 33:21-23). Likewise, when Elijah wanted desperately to hear from God, he was instructed to go out and stand on the mountain "for the Lord is about to pass by" (1 Kings 19:11-13). Then after a storm, earthquake, and fire, he heard God's voice as a "sound of sheer silence."

Both of these are moments of gentleness and protectiveness, whispering power in the midst of terrible commotion and noise. Both of them are what we call *theophanies*, moments when God revealed Himself to His people. *Theophanies* are "those defining moments when God made striking and temporary appearances in the earthly realm to a select individual or group for the purpose of communicating a message."[5] The appearance of God in the burning bush (Exodus 3), the presence of God leading His people in the wilderness with the pillar of fire and smoke (Exodus 13:21-22), the moment God passed by and Moses saw His glory (Exodus 33:21-23)—these are all theophanies.

Though Jesus was fully God and fully human at all times, in some specific moments He aimed to help the disciples realize His identity as God in the flesh. So, when Jesus intended to "pass them by," he was giving His disciples a clarifying moment of His true nature. God was showing Himself to His people.

Reread Mark 6:50. When Jesus walks toward the disciples on the water, what does He say to them?

This story is included in two other Gospels. Write below the words of Jesus as recorded by each Gospel writer:

Matthew 14:27

John 6:20

The language of Jesus' greeting is exactly the same in each account. The words "It is I" were more than clarifying; they were intensely familiar. The exact wording in Greek, *ego ami*, is spoken literally as "I Am." In other words, "Take heart; I Am."

The "I Am" language would have immediately reminded the disciples of God's words spoken to Moses at the burning bush.

Read Exodus 3:13-14. What name did God give to Moses?

I _____ who I _____.

Though we call the setting of this miracle the Sea of Galilee, it's actually a freshwater lake—and not even a large one by many standards. While in other places in Scripture it is called Lake Tiberias or Lake Genneseret, Matthew and Mark make the careful choice to label this body of water over and over again as a sea.

Scholars suggest that by referring to it as a sea, the Gospel writers are evoking the memory of God leading His people through the Red Sea when they escaped slavery in Egypt. Part of the message of this story, then, is that if God could part the waters of the Red Sea for His people to walk through to freedom, Jesus had a similar goal with His life and ministry.

With Jesus' announcement as He walks on the water, the disciples now recognize Him walking over another "sea" on a quest to set us free from the evil forces around and within us.[7] As they witness a great storm calmed by His voice and see Him treading on the seat of evil, they are beginning to realize that this is no magician, powerful man, or even a miracle-working prophet; this is God in the flesh!

3. Do Not Be Afraid

As the disciples are realizing the immense gravity of this moment, learning that their rabbi, teacher, and friend is actually God, they are filled with all kinds of emotions. So Jesus immediately calms them with these words: "Do not be afraid" (Mark 6:50). This is also a common phrase in the theophanies of Scripture, always reassuring people of God's power.

Extra Insight

Galilee is at its broadest point 13 miles long and 8.1 miles wide, while Lake Michigan is 307 miles long by 118 miles wide.[6]

Read the Scriptures below. Beside each, write the recipient of the words "Do not be afraid" and why he or she might have needed to hear those words.

	Recipient	Need
Luke 1:30		
Luke 5:10		
Matthew 28:4-5		

There are many other Scriptures where we find the words "Do not be afraid" or "Do not fear." Look up these phrases in a Bible concordance (online or print), and write below a few of the Scripture references you find:

Do you need to hear these words in some area of your own life right now? If so, why?

God wants us to know that His immense power is matched by immense love, that He will work for our good, and that we can trust Him.

When God reveals Himself, people are filled with awe and fear. But God always reassures us that we don't need to be afraid—not of Him or of anything that comes against us. God wants us to know that His immense power is matched by immense love, that He will work for our good, and that we can trust Him.

Why did Jesus walk on water? Because evil is real; God, who triumphs over evil, is with us; and we need not be afraid.

Jesus is God in the flesh. Because of this, we can expect Jesus' character to reflect the character of God in Scripture. We can expect Jesus' actions to reflect the actions of God in Scripture. We can "take heart" and have no fear because God is with us!

Talk with God

Lord, I am often overwhelmed by how real evil and chaos are in this world. Remind me that You have overcome the world and that Your power and presence are greater than any I see in my surrounding circumstances. Will You speak those words to me again? "Take heart. It is I. Do not be afraid." Amen.

DAY 3: PETER WALKS ON WATER

Read God's Word

²²Immediately Jesus made the disciples get into the boat and go on ahead of him to the other side, while he dismissed the crowd. ²³After he had dismissed them, he went up on a mountainside by himself to pray. Later that night, he was there alone, ²⁴and the boat was already a considerable distance from land, buffeted by the waves because the wind was against it.

²⁵Shortly before dawn Jesus went out to them, walking on the lake. ²⁶When the disciples saw him walking on the lake, they were terrified. "It's a ghost," they said, and cried out in fear.

²⁷But Jesus immediately said to them: "Take courage! It is I. Don't be afraid."

²⁸"Lord, if it's you," Peter replied, "tell me to come to you on the water."

²⁹"Come," he said.

Then Peter got down out of the boat, walked on the water and came toward Jesus. ³⁰But when he saw the wind, he was afraid and, beginning to sink, cried out, "Lord, save me!"

³¹Immediately Jesus reached out his hand and caught him. "You of little faith," he said, "why did you doubt?"

³²And when they climbed into the boat, the wind died down. ³³Then those who were in the boat worshiped him, saying, "Truly you are the Son of God."

(Matthew 14:22-33 NIV)

Reflect and Respond

In the first week of our study I confessed that my curiosity about miracles led me to search the Gospels with a pen in hand, marking M for miracle in the margins. This was the practice that first led me to the desperate moments and the desperate people who preceded each miracle. With each new M in the margins, I learned that desperation precedes a miracle and that each show of God's power is really a show of God's loving and compassionate heart toward those in desperate need.

But there were two miracles in particular that "stumped" me in this regard. These were places where I saw the miracle but, before doing more study, I couldn't see the desperation behind it. The first, which we studied in Week 1, was the miracle of turning water into wine. The mystery of the missing desperation there was solved when we found out just how devastating it would have been for the newly married couple and their families if they had breached their social contract by running out of wine at the week-long wedding celebration. We also discovered that running out of wine was a sign of the long-held desire for a Messiah to come and fill up God's people with abundance and grace.

Today we'll visit the other mystifying miracle, one where the desperation is harder to see at first glance. It may seem familiar, because just yesterday we studied Mark's account of Jesus walking on the water. But today we're going to explore the other telling of this story in the Gospel of Matthew. With this second glance, we'll swing our eyes around from Jesus on the water to the disciples on the boat and find Peter, poised on the edge. Interestingly, Matthew is the only Gospel writer who tells that Peter walked on the water too.

Like other stories of the disciples, Peter is once again at the center of the action. And as in many other stories, we get to see Peter's impetuous nature, which often gets him into trouble—but in this instance gets him into the water to experience something no other disciple ever does.

As I thought about Peter's perspective, I couldn't help but wonder: where was his desperation? What was the "need" that drove him out of the boat, and what was the desperation Jesus was answering with His compassion and miracle-working power? To understand that, I had to search a little deeper into Peter's story.

The waters they sailed on that night were waters where Peter had fished his entire life. The Sea of Galilee was one of those ordinary places for Peter. We all have them in our lives: places where we live day in and day out, going through the everyday, boring motions. Our house. Our commute. Our desk. Our kitchen. Their routines can hold predictable comfort or monotonous boredom. Peter spent many, many nights on the waters of Galilee having the same conversations and going through the same motions for the same small catch.

We forget sometimes that the ordinary places are also where the extraordinary is most likely to happen.

We forget sometimes that the ordinary places are also where the extraordinary is most likely to happen. I once saw a statistic warning that most car accidents occur within just a few miles of our own homes. *Of course*, I thought. *The streets closest to our homes are the ones we drive the most*. Likewise, the probability of getting "struck" by something life-changing is higher in those places where God finds us the most.

The fateful night that Peter and the disciples were out on the boat is one among thousands of nights Peter launched out into those same waters. The sea was Peter's backyard. His desk. His kitchen counter. But that night, in those familiar, ordinary surroundings, something extraordinary happened.

On that night, twelve disciples saw the same strange sight, felt the same terror, heard the same words, and experienced the same awe as Jesus walked effortlessly toward them when, by all natural understandings, He should have sunk. But of the twelve, only one of them spoke up.

Reread Matthew 14:28. Who spoke up, and what did he say?

What do you think possessed Peter to speak those bold words?

It would be wonderful to know exactly what was going through Peter's mind at that moment, but at least in part it must have been this: he wanted to be part of the amazing acts of God that he saw unfolding right in front of his eyes. To take a risk like this, Peter must have been desperate to get out of that boat. But what was Peter desperate for? I'd like to suggest three things.

1. To step out of the ordinary.

Peter was asking to step out onto the waters he knew all too well, the place he had spent many a monotonous night wondering if there was something more than the next wave, the next fish, the next day of doing it all over again. This was the site of Peter's commonplace life, the one he had left to follow Jesus, and he was begging for something more—to know the extraordinary in the ordinary place he knew well.

As followers of Jesus, we all have this seed of desire inside us—or we would never take the risk of following Jesus in the first place.

Where do you sense a desire for God to call you out of the ordinary?

2. To conquer his fears.

Peter was asking to take a risk in a place where he had sought only safety. He had spent his life in awe and respect of these waters. Though he may have been familiar with the water and the boat, he also was familiar with the stories of fishermen who had not made it home from storms such as this one. One wrong step, one big storm, one leaky boat and the sea would become his burial place. In this moment, Peter was asking to step out and tread upon the very thing that had struck fear in his heart his whole life.

Each of us longs for a God who is bigger than the fears that paralyze us and keep us awake at night.

Where do you sense a desire for God to help you conquer your fears?

3. *To walk toward Jesus.*

Notice that Peter's request was not to get out and run aimlessly around on the waves. Peter wasn't out for a thrill. He wasn't out to impress. He was headed one direction: toward Jesus. He asked Jesus for an invitation, saying specifically, "Let me come to you." This wasn't thrill-seeking. It was Christ-seeking.

No matter how long or how closely a disciple has followed Jesus, there is always a deeply held desire to draw closer to Him than ever before.

Where do you sense a desire for God to draw you closer to Jesus?

What next step can you take?

Peter wasn't just asking to defy the laws of nature. He was asking to defy the comfort that kept him imprisoned in everyday routine. He was asking for the courage to defy the fears that had kept him in the boat. He was asking to be closer to Jesus. Expectations had sent him to the boat every day. Fear had kept him in the boat every day. Now he saw his Lord defy the expectations of both the comforts and fears of the world he had always known, and he said, "Lord, if it's real . . . if you're real . . . let me come to you."

Reread Matthew 14:29. How did Jesus respond, and what happened next?

Jesus simply said, "Come," and come Peter did. He put one foot out of the boat and another in front of it, and he was walking on water toward Jesus! Don't miss the exciting meaning of this moment for you and me. If Jesus had just walked on the water by Himself, it would have been enough to tell us that God is powerful beyond the ordinary. But because Peter also walked on water toward Jesus, we know that God wants *us* to be participants in what He's doing in our world—that He wants to empower us to do far more than we could in our own power and strength.

It's one thing to worship a God who has the power to do the miraculous. It's another incredible step to realize that God wants us to share in this journey with Him, to walk alongside Him in ways we could never imagine without His help. On this journey of miracles, God doesn't leave us in the boat as casual observers. He calls us out into the excitement with Him!

When have you sensed God calling you out into the excitement with Him? How might He be calling you to something exciting and new right now?

Peter often is criticized for what happened next. But let's take a closer look.

Reread Matthew 14:30-31. What caused Peter to begin to sink?

What did he cry out?

How quickly did Jesus respond?

What did Jesus say to Peter?

We're often quick to blame Peter for slipping into doubt and fear and beginning to sink, but who wouldn't have a moment of pause upon realizing he or she was breaking the laws of nature? Who wouldn't doubt, being torn by the competing desires to join Jesus and to be safe? As a matter of fact, the Greek word for doubt, *diastase*, means "to attempt to go in two directions at once."[8]

To follow Jesus into scary, uncharted territory means each one of us goes through a kind of internal battle with the two directions we could follow at any moment: to look at the Savior in front of us or the waves beneath us.

> God wants us to share in this journey with Him, to walk alongside Him in ways we could never imagine without His help.

When have you stepped out to follow Jesus only to experience an internal battle of doubt and fear?

Peter's story makes it clear that even the closest disciple in the middle of the most amazing display of God's strength will be torn between those two desires: the desire to let Jesus call the shots and the desire to move back toward the safety and familiarity of controlling our own lives, even if it means a boring life of boat-dwelling.

"Lord, save me," Peter cried, and then *immediately* Jesus reached out His hand. Thank God for that "immediately"! Without delay or hesitation Jesus responded by reaching where Peter was—doubt or no doubt—and saving Him once again.

> **Being saved by Jesus means seeing that the waves are too big for us but knowing that nothing is too big for Him.**

When we talk about being "saved" by Jesus, we are essentially saying this is our story too. We were sinking in something that was over our heads with our eyes focused on the peril and our fear, but we knew somewhere in the back of our minds that Jesus was right there, even if we weren't looking at Him at first. Being saved by Jesus means seeing that the waves are too big for us but knowing that nothing is too big for Him.

On another occasion when the disciples woke a sleeping Jesus and begged Him to still the storm, they were asking Him to take them from a place of danger to safety. But when Peter asked to get out of the boat, he was asking to move from a place of safety to danger. He was desperate to be desperate, and he got his wish. The waves were a place that challenged his fear to the utmost, and the same waves were a place that proved the willingness of his Savior to reach out and save him in a tight spot, even when the sinking was his own fault.

It was when he was sinking in the waves that Peter learned a lesson he would later need to draw on again and again: that "Christ does not fail even those who fail him."[9]

When and how have you learned this lesson?

God wants our attention fully on Him and will stop at nothing to get it. But He also wants us to know that there is a life out there greater than the ordinary that we can be part of. Miracles of every kind, whether spectacular or more everyday, invite us out of the boat and into the journey with Jesus. I hope that the encounter we've explored today will give you the boldness to trust Jesus more and the courage to say, "Lord, if it's you—if all of this is real—tell me to come to you!"

Talk with God

Jesus, witnessing Your miracles is stirring up a deep desire in me for something more than the ordinary. Call me out of the boat of my comfort and routine to follow You in ways I could never dream in my own strength or power. When I doubt and sink, reach out and grab me again. When I witness You doing great things, remind me to say again, "Lord, if it's You, let me come with You!" Amen.

DAY 4: THE RHYTHM OF REST

Read God's Word

¹Thus the heavens and the earth were finished, and all their multitude. ²And on the seventh day God finished the work that he had done, and he rested on the seventh day from all the work that he had done. ³So God blessed the seventh day and hallowed it, because on it God rested from all the work that he had done in creation.

(Genesis 2:1-3)

⁴⁵Immediately Jesus made his disciples get into the boat and go on ahead of him to Bethsaida, while he dismissed the crowd. ⁴⁶After leaving them, he went up on a mountainside to pray.

(Mark 6:45-46 NIV)

Reflect and Respond

My first winter living outside of Texas was a rude (and cold!) awakening. You may be from some frozen tundra such as Greenland or Michigan and think Kentucky winters are nothing. But since I had grown up in a place where the temperature only occasionally dipped below freezing, my first true winter season was a tough one.

Then, in the long, dark days of a year with record-breaking snow for Central Kentucky, God provided. I was invited to speak on a retreat, which happened to be held onboard a five-day Caribbean cruise!

Let me tell you, that was not a difficult assignment.

I won't bore you with stories of sandy beaches and five-course dinners with two desserts—not to mention a group of two hundred fantastic Christian women who woke early for Bible study and stayed up late for worship every day. The part I want to share with you is what happened when the cruise was over, specifically what happened to me when I got off the ship. When my feet touched terra firma back at the port we were returning to, the ground seemed to tilt beneath me as if it was swaying, rocking side to side like the deck of a ship.

While I never got seasick aboard the ship for five days, back on dry land I suddenly had trouble keeping my balance. I returned from a sunny paradise to winter-stricken Kentucky and found that I had to hold on to things to keep from swaying side to side or even falling over.

It was kind of amusing at first, but the vertigo, headaches, fatigue, and inability to look at a book or a screen without getting dizzy weren't funny for long. When I stood to preach a week later, swaying and holding on to the pulpit, I was worried someone was going to demand a sobriety test!

I was suffering from a condition called Mal de Debarquement Syndrome, a very French way of saying "the sickness after disembarking." Sometimes described simply as land-sickness, it means that even though you're standing on solid ground, your brain still thinks you're moving; having so adjusted to the motion of the boat, it has a hard time stopping. In short, my body had been in motion for so long that it had forgotten how to be still.

Stillness is not something most of us are good at. Our world today is one of continual motion. Many of us are in the business of busyness. Grown-ups are busy. Families are busy. Churches are busy. We run from one event and commitment to the next without much time to stop. Our bodies have been in motion for so long they sometimes forget how to be still. And if we're not careful, it will make us sick.

I'm not just sharing the story of my motion sickness here to fit in with our theme of encounters on the water. Jesus lived out a pattern of action, rest, engagement, and reflection. In His humanity we find times where Jesus stopped and rested before or after important and tiring action in ministry. Today we read a story of Jesus staying behind to rest and take a break even from His disciples. But we also find that the rhythm of rest is part of God's character and part of the Creation story.

God created us to live with a rhythm of rest.

God created us to live with a rhythm of rest. If you look at the story of Creation as told in the first chapter of Genesis, you'll find a poetic story that captures this rhythm so well. For the first six days of Creation, the great masterpiece of Creation is described in an almost musical beat, with cadence and tempo, repeating words such as these:

Evening and morning

The first day, the second day, the third day, and so on

And God saw that it was good . . . (and on the last day God saw that everything was very good)

You could almost set a metronome to the reading of this first chapter of the Bible. There is such poetry here, such artistry in the telling. It's meant to mirror the artistry of the creation described. But it's only when you hear the rhythm of the first six days that you realize what happens so clearly on the seventh day, the last day of Creation, when that rhythm stops. On that day God finished. God rested. God blessed. That's it. No evening and morning, no good or very good. There's a very distinct feeling of putting on the brakes.

If Creation is the song of God's rhythms of creative work, then that seventh day called Sabbath is the rest in the score of music. If you play a piece of music and don't read the rests, you mess the whole thing up. But that's what we tend to do: try to experience God's good creation without Sabbath rest.

Sabbath comes from the Hebrew word *sabbat*, which simply means "to cease," and the rhythm of stopping for one day of the week, just as God stopped—the rest at the end of the melody of the week—defined the song of the lives of God's people. Observing the Sabbath, or ceasing, was so important that it was listed in the Ten Commandments.

Read Exodus 20:8-10 in the margin. What are we to cease from doing on the Sabbath?

In verse 8, what word is used to describe this practice of rest?

> [8]*"Remember the Sabbath day by keeping it holy.* [9]*Six days you shall labor and do all your work,* [10]*but the seventh day is a sabbath to the Lord your God. On it you shall not do any work, neither you, nor your son or daughter, nor your male or female servant, nor your animals, nor any foreigner residing in your towns."*
>
> *(Exodus 20:8-10 NIV)*

This is the commandment we break far more than any of the others. We are a people so in motion that it's hard to stop sometimes. It's a bit ironic that God, who can never be exhausted, chose to rest, while we humans, who do get exhausted, often choose not to rest.

Do you struggle to take time to rest on a regular basis? If so, what are some of the things that make it difficult for you to rest?

Ceasing activity to be with God on one day changes what happens *on* that day, but it also deeply affects what happens *in us* on the other six days. Giving our time to God in this way has the same effect as tithing a portion of our money: it reminds us that all we have is God's, and it sets our priorities for not just one portion of our assets but for all that we hold in stewardship for God.

Ceasing activity to be with God on one day changes what happens *on* that day, but it also deeply affects what happens *in us* on the other six days.

God wants us to offer not just one day a week for Him but all of our days. Creating rhythms of rest where we cease our work and frantic activity to stop and simply "be" doesn't have to wait for a single day. In fact, it shouldn't!

Jesus set the example for us. He certainly honored the Sabbath, but He also found other times to stop, ceasing motion and ministry, and connect in a deep way with His heavenly Father. Let's look at some of Jesus' rhythms of moving and stopping—of action and reflection.

The water miracles that we're focusing on this week happen around some of the busiest times of ministry for Jesus.

Read Mark 4:1 in the margin. Where is Jesus teaching? Why does He move out onto the water?

Jesus began to teach by the lake. The crowd that gathered around him was so large that he got into a boat and sat in it out on the lake, while all the people were along the shore at the water's edge.
(Mark 4:1 NIV)

When He is done teaching, Jesus commands the disciples to leave the shore and sail across the lake, leaving the crowds behind. Here's where we again encounter those words about Jesus' nap in the storm: "But he was in the stern, asleep on the cushion" (Mark 4:38). Jesus was so tired, evidently, that He was able to sleep through a storm that frightened seasoned fishermen! I love that Jesus took naps. If the Lord of the universe could lay down His head and rest, it gives us great permission to stop and rest as well.

In Mark 6, we see that the crowds are again overwhelming, so Jesus calls the disciples away to a quiet place to get some rest. But the crowds follow them, and Jesus has such compassion on their needs that He teaches them many things and miraculously feeds them (vv. 30-44). We're told that after feeding the five thousand, Jesus sent His disciples ahead by boat.

Reread Mark 6:45-46. After the disciples left, where did Jesus go and what did He do?

> If the Lord of the universe could lay down His head and rest, it gives us great permission to stop and rest as well.

I imagine that there was no end to the work Jesus could have done. He could have stayed with the crowds, continually meeting the never-ending needs of those brought to Him. He could have stayed with the disciples, giving them much-needed instruction and answering questions until He had no more voice. Instead, He knew that He needed time alone with His heavenly Father.

Look up these verses about some other times Jesus goes away to a quiet place to rest and be with the Father. What do you learn from these times? Glance at what He's doing just before and just after them. What do you think is the reason or purpose behind these times?

Mark 1:35

Matthew 26:36-46

Luke 5:15-16

Jesus not only knew that He needed rest from the demands of the crowd, He also knew that the disciples would need time away as well. Repeatedly, He would direct them to retreat from the crowds for some time alone together.

Read Mark 6:30-31 in the margin. Have you ever sensed Jesus nudging you to time alone with God—maybe even to a deserted place? If so, describe that experience:

Jesus had a rhythm of rest and restoration that involved being actively and fully engaged with large groups of people, but that also required Him to go away to quiet places to rest and be alone with His Father. When we hesitate to stop and rest, it's as if we're saying that we are more important or our work is more needed than the work of Jesus. Friend, you and I are not the Messiah! We can lay our work aside and spend time receiving rest, prayer, and care from God just as Jesus did.

Do you have a regular rhythm of rest and restoration in your life? If so, describe it below. If not, what is keeping you from creating this rhythm?

I grew up in Texas, and whenever someone said, "Let's go dancing," I always knew what they meant. They didn't mean ballroom or swing or salsa dancing. They meant the Texas two-step. The strange thing about the Texas two-step

> *30The apostles gathered around Jesus and reported to him all they had done and taught. 31Then, because so many people were coming and going that they did not even have a chance to eat, he said to them, "Come with me by yourselves to a quiet place and get some rest."*
> *(Mark 6:30-31 NIV)*

Jesus had a rhythm of rest and restoration.... When we hesitate to stop and rest, it's as if we're saying that we are more important or our work is more needed than the work of Jesus.

is that it's actually a dance that has *three* steps. I was taught to say under my breath with the steps, "Quick, quick, *slow*. Quick, quick, *slow*. Quick, quick *slow*." Though there are three steps, there are only two types of steps; thus it is called the two-step.

Now, here's the secret to two-stepping. You can't leave out a step. If you forget the slow step, things don't go well. You tend to trip over your partner and look foolish. Ask me how I know!

If you leave out the slow step, you really don't even have a dance anymore. Lots of quick steps with no slow step isn't a dance; it's a race. Imagine if you invited someone to dance and they started running. I'm sure that's not exactly the desired response to an invitation to dance.

God's command to rest is an invitation to dance—an invitation for you to return to His rhythm and observe the rests in the song of your life. Many passages in the Bible speak of this invitation to find rest in God's presence and how this affects our lives.

> **Read the following Scriptures and write some words from each to remind yourself of God's desire to meet with you.**
>
> Matthew 6:5-6

Psalm 27:7

Isaiah 40:31

> **When we accept God's invitation to rest in His presence, we experience a divine reboot.**

When we accept God's invitation to rest in His presence, we experience a divine reboot. We're reminded that we are finite creatures with limits and our worth is not in our work. We realize that our relationship with God is meant to be a dance, not a race.

Listen, we're all bad at this to start with. If we were great at it, God wouldn't have had to make it a command! If we knew how to do this instinctively, we wouldn't need the example of Jesus, who drew apart again and again.

We all get tired, burned out, fatigued. But Jesus told us where to go with that fatigue.

> **Read Matthew 11:28 in the margin. Where are we to go with our fatigue, and what will we receive in return?**

"Come to me, all you that are weary and are carrying heavy burdens, and I will give you rest."
(Matthew 11:28)

Jesus calls us to come to Him. And He promises that when we do, He will give us the gift of rest.

Because we see Jesus stopping periodically for rest, prayer, and reflection, we know that we must too. Sabbath is solid ground in a shifting sea of life. It's a way of giving one day to steady our nerves and remind ourselves again that we belong to God and are useful to Him because of who we are, not what we do. Sabbath rest helps us recalibrate, reboot, retreat in a way that will remind us on every other day to come apart with God to enjoy Him. It helps us find ourselves on steady ground again. And that is something we all desperately need.

End your study time today by reading the Extra Insight and writing a plan below for some times of rest and retreat this week. Include both shorter moments and a plan for Sabbath.

Extra Insight

Sabbath can look like slowing down or stopping something you normally do (tecÚology, meetings, e-mail), as well as enjoying time with God, family, and friends. Sabbath isn't about adding a burden to your schedule but helping you release your burdens to God.

Talk with God

God, I am in need of rest. This is no accident, but a purposeful way You made me. Let me hear those words from You that the disciples heard: "Come away with Me to a quiet place to rest." Help me to listen and obey. Amen.

DAY 5: SEQUELS— THE MIRACULOUS CATCH

Read God's Word

¹*After these things Jesus showed himself again to the disciples by the Sea of Tiberias; and he showed himself in this way.* ²*Gathered there together were Simon Peter, Thomas called the Twin, Nathanael of Cana in Galilee, the sons of Zebedee, and two others of his disciples.* ³*Simon Peter said to them, "I am going fishing." They said to him, "We will go with you." They went out and got into the boat, but that night they caught nothing.*

⁴*Just after daybreak, Jesus stood on the beach; but the disciples did not know that it was Jesus.* ⁵*Jesus said to them, "Children, you have no fish, have you?" They answered him, "No." * ⁶*He said to them, "Cast the net to the right side of the boat,*

and you will find some." So they cast it, and now they were not able to haul it in because there were so many fish. ⁷That disciple whom Jesus loved said to Peter, "It is the Lord!" When Simon Peter heard that it was the Lord, he put on some clothes, for he was naked, and jumped into the sea. ⁸But the other disciples came in the boat, dragging the net full of fish, for they were not far from the land, only about a hundred yards off.

⁹When they had gone ashore, they saw a charcoal fire there, with fish on it, and bread. ¹⁰Jesus said to them, "Bring some of the fish that you have just caught." ¹¹So Simon Peter went aboard and hauled the net ashore, full of large fish, a hundred fifty-three of them; and though there were so many, the net was not torn.

(John 21:1-11)

Reflect and Respond

The movie business loves a good sequel. *Mission Impossible*. *Toy Story*. *Star Wars*. *Rocky*.

Once an audience is hooked on a particular storyline and has fallen in love with a set of characters, it's easy to rope them in to a return visit to the theater for Part Two or Part Three or even Part Six! There's a reason we love sequels: they give us the thrill of both the familiar and the unknown, all in one package. Sitting in a darkened theater and hearing well-known and well-loved theme music begin, we know we're in for something great—we just don't yet know what the adventure will be!

The miracle that we're looking at today seems like a sequel to an earlier encounter with Jesus. This miracle is the last one in the Gospels, performed even after Jesus' death and resurrection, but I'm including it here because it happened on the water. And like the other water miracles, its original audience was the disciples alone.

In this case, the disciples are approaching the end of the toughest week of their lives. They watched their Savior and friend be arrested, tortured, and killed. And then, in a huge plot twist, He rose from the dead and appeared to them twice after that. You might say they are a little bit disoriented! Nothing has prepared them for the last few days of extreme lows and highs, moments of devastation and hope—and probably a lot of confusion.

What do you do when your life is in a state of confusion?

Many of us seek out something familiar. We go to a place that brings us comfort, or go talk to a person whose presence feels reassuring. I had a roommate who used to watch the movie *The Little Princess* every time she was sick or down. It comforted her to hear the familiar lines of her favorite movie. If we walked by her room and heard the lines from this movie playing, we knew she was in a bad place and trying to cheer herself up.

So, what did the disciples do when life seemed out of control? They went fishing!

The disciples have sometimes been criticized for returning to fishing so soon after Easter. If Jesus called them to leave their nets, why are they back fishing again? Some have even wondered if they have given up on the ministry they've been called to and trained for, going back to their old lives.

I can see why the disciples might have headed to the water when they didn't know where else to go. Imagine if your Lord has been crucified and you are longing to hear His voice. Where do you go? If you want Him to call you, instruct you, and work miracles on your behalf, you might just head back to the place where you first were called and instructed, the place you saw Him perform miracles. You might go back to the boat.

We're told at the beginning of the story that the disciples have been fishing all night and have caught nothing—which, if you've ever been fishing, you know is pretty typical. Waiting and catching nothing is probably the most common part of the fishing experience.

They are discouraged and are pulling their nets up when suddenly a figure calls out to them from the shore.

Reread John 21:5-6. What does Jesus tell them to do, and what happens next?

When they obey and suddenly there are so many fish they can't even pull in the nets, a light bulb goes off. *This has happened before*!

The disciples begin to recall the story we read in Week 2, when Jesus called the disciples (Luke 5). As you'll recall, several fishermen had spent all night fishing with no catch. Jesus used the boat as a floating platform to teach from and then gave them almost the same instructions. Let's review those instructions together.

Write Luke 5:4 below:

The story of the abundant catch that followed got the fishermen's attention, to say the least, and Jesus captured their attention into an opportunity to call them to follow Him as His disciples.

God uses the abundance in our lives to get our attention and then turn it to Him.

Now, as the resurrected Lord appears as a distant figure on the shore, the disciples once again know it is Jesus because of the abundance. Unlike the story from Luke, when they were relative strangers to Jesus and His remarkable gifts, here in John they have been with Him throughout His ministry. They've seen Him change water into abundant wine; they've witnessed the five loaves and two fish become an abundant meal for a crowd. And now this abundant catch has "Jesus" written all over it. This time they even count the catch!

According to John 21:11, how many fish did they catch?

Fishermen always measure and count. It's the only way to tell a good fish story! Clearly the abundance has captured their attention, but it's not what keeps their attention.

As we learned earlier in our study, in John's Gospel miraculous events—healings, exorcisms, resurrections, acts of abundance—are never referred to as miracles. No, John calls them signs. Signs have no value except to point to something else, and the miracles all point to Jesus.

The abundance isn't the point; the point is Jesus. The abundance, the signs, only exist to point us to Him.

What are some signs of God's abundance in your life, and how do they point you to Jesus?

Most of the sequels I see these days (with two small children) are animated movies. One that my children adored was *Finding Dory*, the sequel to Walt Disney Pictures' *Finding Nemo*.

Finding Dory is about a fish (appropriate for a fishing story!) who is on a search for her family. She has short-term memory loss and has been separated from her parents, but she doesn't know how or where. The movie is about her search for them and the journey on which it takes her.

When Dory is little, her parents are aware of the danger of her getting lost and not being able to remember her way home. So they look for a tool that will get her attention and point her back to them. Dory loves shells, so her parents create trails of shells and teach her to notice them and follow them back to home, back to them.

In the most poignant scene of the movie, Dory, having been lost for years in the vast ocean, follows a trail of shells and finds at the end of it her loving parents, waiting there for her. It's a heartwarming reunion, but it gets even better. When the scene zooms out, we see multiple trails radiating out from their house like the rays of the sun. Every trail points back to home, back to the place where those who love Dory best are waiting for her. Her parents had prepared in abundance for the purpose of leading her home.

In a similar way, God uses the abundance in our lives to get our attention and then turn it to Him. If we keep our eyes on the abundant things, we are missing the point. They are not signs that point to themselves but abundant trails that lead us home to God.

Abundance always gets our attention. If Jesus is associated with abundance, I'm sure there is some kind of abundance we'd all like to ask for. "Yes, Lord," we say, "I'd like an abundance of_____." Funds. Chocolate. Vacations. Well-mannered children. Job offers. Compliments. You fill in the blank.

But sometimes the trails leading us to seek Jesus are a different kind of abundance—abundance of need, abundance of worry, or abundance of realization that we just aren't making it on our own. While God may not be the author of adversity, He certainly won't waste a sign if He can turn it to point you to Him. All of these things can point you to the One who has been searching for you all along, lining up signs to direct you to Him.

When has an abundance of need, worry, or insufficiency pointed you to Jesus?

You may remember that Peter's response in the first abundant catch story is different from his response the second time.

Read the verses in the margin, and note Peter's different responses below:

Luke 5:8

John 21:7

The first time, the miraculous presence of a holy God causes Peter to notice his own sin. But later, after all they've been through together, Peter actually drops everything, including the catch! He swims away from the huge catch of

> **While God may not be the author of adversity, He certainly won't waste a sign if He can turn it to point you to Him.**

> *"Go away from me, Lord, for I am a sinful man!"*
> *(Luke 5:8)*

> *That disciple whom Jesus loved said to Peter, "It is the Lord!" When Simon Peter heard that it was the Lord, he put on some clothes, for he was naked, and jumped into the sea.*
> *(John 21:7)*

fish and toward the Lord. Peter is more aware of his own sin than ever before because the last time he saw Jesus alive, he was denying Him. But as much as he knows his own sin, he knows even more the abundance of grace and forgiveness that is in Jesus. It is that abundance that inspires him not to wait for the boat to row ashore but to swim to Jesus Himself.

Today you've considered the abundance you've seen in your own life—the abundance of things that have caught your attention the way the glinting light on a thousand fish scales caught the disciples' eyes, as well as the abundance of needs and desperate moments when you've needed Him the most. And I'm just as sure there has been an abundance of ways He has helped you through, an abundance of moments when His strength has been enough in your weakness, and an abundance of things you can give thanks for.

Whether you're facing an abundance of reasons to believe in God's power or an abundance of desire to look for those reasons, follow that trail. Let the good and the bad point you to Jesus.

The psalmist says, "Surely goodness and mercy shall follow me / all the days of my life" (Psalm 23:6). The Hebrew word for *follow* in this passage literally means "chase." Goodness and mercy are chasing after you, hunting you down, trying to find you. The irony for those of us who think we have been "searching" for God is that He has been chasing us all along!

Talk with God

Lord, the things that trouble me are abundant. They make me cry out to You in desperation, for I know I am weak and You are strong. But Lord, the abundance of beauty and blessing in my life also calls my attention to You. Thank You for Your great faithfulness and loving-kindness. Whichever I find in abundance today, help it to turn me to You, O God, my rock and my redeemer. Amen.

VIDEO VIEWER GUIDE: WEEK 3

Mark 4:35-37

Mark 4:38

Psalm 22:1-2

God is not ___distant___ at all; He's literally in the same ___boat___ with us.

God is in the boat with us even when it's too ___dark___ to see Him.

Mark 6:45-52

There are times we are desperate to be ___desperate___ to take a ___Risk___ for God's sake that will change the world for the better.

What holy risk does God have for you next?

Week 4

JESUS OUR HEALER

Our Broken Places in His Healing Hands

DAY 1: HEALING THE LEPER

Read God's Word

¹²*While Jesus was in one of the towns, a man came along who was covered with leprosy. When he saw Jesus, he fell with his face to the ground and begged him, "Lord, if you are willing, you can make me clean."*

¹³*Jesus reached out his hand and touched the man. "I am willing," he said. "Be clean!" And immediately the leprosy left him.*

¹⁴*Then Jesus ordered him, "Don't tell anyone, but go, show yourself to the priest and offer the sacrifices that Moses commanded for your cleansing, as a testimony to them."*

¹⁵*Yet the news about him spread all the more, so that crowds of people came to hear him and to be healed of their sicknesses. ¹⁶But Jesus often withdrew to lonely places and prayed.*

(Luke 5:12-16 NIV)

Reflect and Respond

One of God's characteristics as Creator that I've always been most grateful for is that He stays interested in and engaged with His creation. Although God could have cried "Done!" on the seventh day of Creation and walked away—or could have easily given up on us during our multiple mess-ups throughout human history—the fact is that He never leaves us or gives up on us. In my own life, I've reached points of discouragement so deep that I was sure things were broken beyond repair, but the reminder that my Creator was still waiting to heal, restore, and remedy the injustice and brokenness around me kept me from giving up many times. No matter how broken people or situations may seem, nothing is beyond God's healing hand.

As we see in the Gospels, most of the miracles Jesus performed were healings. One-fifth of the Gospels—or 727, of the 3,779 verses—concern healing in one way or another. That's a remarkable amount of emphasis on healing.[1]

Why did Jesus spend so much time healing people and talking about healing? One obvious reason is that He had compassion on people who were sick—people whose lives were broken and whose hearts were desperate. He had the power to change their lives, and so He did. But there's an even bigger picture of God's heart here that reveals to us how He wants us, His children, to live: restored and whole.

If we look at this bigger picture of God's purposes for the world as communicated in Scripture, we see that His hopes do not include sickness or

³*And I heard a loud voice from the throne saying,*

"See, the home of God is among mortals.
He will dwell with them;
they will be his peoples,
and God himself will be with them;
⁴*he will wipe every tear from their eyes.*
Death will be no more;
mourning and crying and pain will be no more,
for the first things have passed away."

⁵*And the one who was seated on the throne said, "See, I am making all things new." Also he said, "Write this, for these words are trustworthy and true."*

(Revelation 21:3-5)

death. The story of Creation painted in the first two chapters of Genesis shows a harmonious existence with no sickness or death or brokenness of any kind. Even the relationship between God and His people and their relationships with each other are unblemished by any kind of shame or division.

The story of God's restored world in the very last chapters of Revelation reveals a remarkably similar picture.

Read Revelation 21:3-5 in the margin. What message is given at the end about pain, death, or relational brokenness?

If we want to understand God's heart for healing, we need to remember that He does not desire pain, sickness, or death for His people. Those things entered the world through human sin and evil, and the chapters between the first of Genesis and the last of Revelation show God's work of stamping out these things and reconciling His people to Himself. The Revelation passage promises us that God ultimately will accomplish this goal of no more death, mourning, crying, or pain. Total restoration.

What thoughts and feelings do you have when you imagine a world with no sickness, death, mourning, crying, or pain?

Since Jesus was God walking in flesh on the earth, we can see the ultimate purposes of God through Jesus' actions, words, and relationships. This means that if we want to know what the heart of God looks like, we can see it in the life and ministry of Jesus. So, if someone ever tells you that sickness or pain or death came from God, just look at Jesus' life and you'll see that He never used His miraculous power to cause anyone sickness or pain or death. Actually, whenever He encountered these things, He set about to reverse them. Each personal healing Jesus performed is a small picture of God's grand plan for His creation.

This week we'll look together at five healing stories to see what we can learn about the heart of God through Jesus' healing ministry, and today we begin with the story of a man with a skin disease. This man who came to Jesus for healing had leprosy, and it wasn't a mild case.

Read Luke 5:12. What does Luke tell us about the man's leprosy?

When we hear that this man was *covered* with leprosy, we might think about how much he must have suffered. But in some ways, it didn't matter how mild or severe his condition was. In those days even a tiny spot of leprosy changed the course of a person's life forever. Leviticus 13 is full of guidelines for how to determine if a person has leprosy (some translations use the phrase "defiling skin disease"). It was the job of the priests to diagnose the disease; and if it was leprosy, the person's entire life was altered.

Read Leviticus 13:45-46. What were the requirements for persons diagnosed with leprosy? How would this disease affect their lives?

One source sheds some light on the plight of persons with this dreaded skin disease: "Lepers were thus outcasts from the rest of society, the kind of people most healthy people preferred to ignore. Touching a leper was forbidden, . . . and most people would have been revolted by the thought of it."[2] So, we see that leprosy was not only a physical condition; it was a "social disease" as well, preventing others from living with those who were infected—or even touching them.

Those with leprosy were forced to live together just outside the city gate and were required to shout "Unclean!" if anyone approached them to protect the other person from coming too close. Lepers also had to change their physical appearance to show that they were outcasts, so that no stranger could miss the fact that they were unclean. Because a leper was considered spiritually unclean, touching someone with leprosy would make you spiritually unclean as well; and that would require you to go for a check-up and spiritual cleansing by a priest. Your entire world—physical, social, spiritual, and cultural—would be turned upside down by the diagnosis of leprosy.

With this understanding of the requirements for persons with leprosy, it is shocking that this man did not keep the prescribed distance but approached Jesus. He must have heard about or witnessed Jesus' healing power, and so he chose to take a huge risk.

The story is told in all three Synoptic Gospels. Read each Scripture and record how the man's actions or approach is described:

Matthew 8:1-2 _____

> God's desire was not pain, sickness, or death for His people. . . . The chapters between the first of Genesis and the last of Revelation show God's work of stamping out these things and reconciling His people to Himself.

Extra Insight

Unlike our modern understanding of leprosy, which we now call Hansen's disease, the biblical diagnosis of leprosy encompassed many different skin diseases.

Mark 1:40 _____

Luke 5:12 _____

> We need the boldness to go to Jesus in our desperation and the humility to know we need His mercy when we get there.

In each of these accounts, the man came close to Jesus and lowered himself. Luke recounts that he lowered himself so much that he put his face on the ground and begged, throwing himself at Jesus' feet.

Don't miss this powerful combination of boldness and humility! Because of his diagnosis and social shame, the man was supposed to stay at a distance from others. According to popular understanding, he was unclean, unworthy, and undeserving of Jesus' attention. But in his desperation, he became bold and willing to ask for Jesus' help. Yet when he boldly approached Jesus, his posture wasn't one of arrogance or entitlement but humility—*begging*. The combination of these two postures of boldness and humility was powerful then, and it is powerful now. We need the boldness to go to Jesus in our desperation and the humility to know we need His mercy when we get there.

The Gospel writer Luke especially loved to tell stories of people who placed themselves at the feet of Jesus by kneeling or humbling themselves.

Read the verses below and fill in the information. (You may need to read surrounding verses to help you determine why there is humility in each instance.)

	Person	Action	Reason for Their Humility
Luke 10:39			
Luke 5:8			
Luke 7:36-50			

This combination of the boldness to approach Jesus and the humility to bow before Him is the posture of prayer. It's the posture of abandonment in the presence of the Holy. It's a posture of the heart, not just of the knees. And it's a posture that pleases God. God loves our willingness to come to Him and ask for what we need in the same way that a caring parent loves to hear a humble and genuine need from his or her child.

So, the man at Jesus' feet cried out in bold humility: "Lord, if you are willing, you can make me clean" (Luke 5:12 NIV).

How have you experienced boldness in your approach to God?

How have you experienced humility in your approach to God?

Now, hold your breath as you read again what happened next, because it's shocking: "Jesus reached out his hand and touched the man" (Luke 5:13 NIV).

He *touched* this man—this contaminated man who was thought to be unclean and would defile anyone he touched; this lonely man who possibly had not been touched by anyone in years. There are healings of leprosy in the Old Testament, such as in Numbers 12 and 2 Kings 5; but even in those situations, Moses and Elisha didn't dare touch the persons being healed. Touch means connection, relationship, acknowledgment—and these are hallmarks of Jesus' healing ministry. Don't miss the fact that Jesus reached out and touched this man *while he was still covered in leprosy*—while he was unclean with a disease that everyone would now say Jesus was unclean with as well.

I love the lines repeated every time we take Communion in my church. Once we have confessed our sins together, the officiating pastor lifts his or her hands over the congregation and says,

> Hear the good news:
> > Christ died for us while we were yet sinners;
> > that proves God's love toward us.
> In the name of Jesus Christ, you are forgiven.[3]

The first part of this statement echoes the words of Romans 5:2. This is the kind of declaration Jesus was giving with His touch of the leprous man. Just as Jesus took a step toward him, touched him, and made him clean, so Jesus died for us before we were forgiven. Before we were worthy or deserving, Christ took a step toward us and gave His life for us.

The understanding of leprosy was that it was too contagious to risk touching or even being near the infected person. But Jesus' "cleanness" was more contagious than the man's uncleanness. And this is good news for us, too! Jesus' holiness is always more powerful than the problems He encounters in our lives. There is nothing in us—or in anyone else—that is so damaged Christ will not lovingly touch when we ask with bold humility.

Jesus' holiness is always more powerful than the problems He encounters in our lives.

What "uncleanness" in your life do you need to present to Jesus right now with bold humility? Write a prayer below asking for Jesus' healing touch:

The passage tells us that *immediately* the leprosy left the man and he was healed.

Reread Luke 5:14. What instructions did Jesus give the man?

Jesus' goal for us is always more than a physical cure; it's restoration in community with others and with God Himself.

By sending him to the priest, Jesus was reconnecting the man with his community. Jesus healed his disease, but now the man needed to be declared clean to be restored in relationship to those he loved. Here's another amazing truth: Jesus' goal for us is always more than a physical cure; it's restoration in community with others and with God Himself. Just like the picture painted in Genesis and Revelation, God is always working toward a restored, healed, and whole world.

At the end of the story, Jesus called on the man to give testimony to those in his community of what had happened. Jesus knew that when we tell others how our lives have been touched by God, it makes the "cleanness" even more contagious because their lives are touched as well.

Now that we've begun our exploration of Jesus' healing miracles, I hope you're excited by what you've found in this first story. Don't miss this personal takeaway: God wants *you* to approach Him with bold humility and offer Him your needs. He wants you to know that there's nothing so damaged in your life (or the lives of others) that would deter Him from touching you. *Nothing*.

Then, as you experience the joy of seeing your life change in His hands, remember to testify to those around you. Your joy will be contagious!

Talk with God

Lord, I want to approach You with bold humility and humble boldness. I know I need Your touch on my life and on the lives of those who have my heart. I also praise You for the times Your contagious holiness has overwhelmed the sick places in my life and made them well. Help me to tell Your story! Amen.

DAY 2: CARRIED TO JESUS

Read God's Word

¹A few days later, when Jesus again entered Capernaum, the people heard that he had come home. ²They gathered in such large numbers that there was no room left, not even outside the door, and he preached the word to them. ³Some men came, bringing to him a paralyzed man, carried by four of them. ⁴Since they could not get him to Jesus because of the crowd, they made an opening in the roof above Jesus by digging through it and then lowered the mat the man was lying on. ⁵When Jesus saw their faith, he said to the paralyzed man, "Son, your sins are forgiven."

⁶Now some teachers of the law were sitting there, thinking to themselves, ⁷"Why does this fellow talk like that? He's blaspheming! Who can forgive sins but God alone?"

⁸Immediately Jesus knew in his spirit that this was what they were thinking in their hearts, and he said to them, "Why are you thinking these things? ⁹Which is easier: to say to this paralyzed man, 'Your sins are forgiven,' or to say, 'Get up, take your mat and walk'? ¹⁰But I want you to know that the Son of Man has authority on earth to forgive sins." So he said to the man, ¹¹"I tell you, get up, take your mat and go home." ¹²He got up, took his mat and walked out in full view of them all. This amazed everyone and they praised God, saying, "We have never seen anything like this!"

(Mark 2:1-12 NIV)

Reflect and Respond

Our small group had been meeting in my living room every Thursday night for a few months. There were singles and couples, parents and non-parents. This group of fun-loving, smart, engaging believers in Jesus was digging deeper each week both into God's Word and into relationship with one another. Each week the questions grew deeper and more personal and the conversation and fun got louder.

At the end of our time together each week we would ask for prayer requests. Unlike the rest of our time together, the prayer request time seemed to be the quietest point of our gatherings. We were in that stage of community where we were hesitantly learning just how vulnerable we wanted to be with our own deepest concerns and needs. One young married couple spoke up hesitantly, asking us to pray for an "unspoken" prayer request.

We knew what the word *unspoken* meant: they needed prayer but weren't comfortable sharing what it was about. The next week, they lifted up the same request. This went on for several weeks, but they didn't elaborate; and honestly,

no one in the group had the courage to ask for more information. Then one week they didn't show up. The next week they were absent as well. I called the wife to ask if everything was OK. She hesitated for a moment, took a deep breath, and then said, "We're getting a divorce. We've tried everything and it's just never going to work. We won't be coming back to the group."

I could hear the pain and struggle in her voice as we talked. As I listened to my friend and asked questions about what they had been through, she admitted that this was the first they had told anyone. They hadn't spoken out loud of the situation to their family or friends or our group. They hadn't been to our pastor for help or sought marriage counseling. I began to wonder what she meant by "we've tried everything" when they hadn't tried the support of the community around them. The more isolated they had become in their secret struggle, the worse it had become. My heart broke for them.

One of the hardest things in life is to admit that we need help. None of us likes to confess to others that we don't have it all together or that we don't know how to handle a problem. And yet most of us would be willing, even eager, to help if someone came to us with the same need. We are much more comfortable being the ones who help others than needing help ourselves.

The healing story we're focusing on today is about the remarkable love of a group of friends. There's so much we don't know about them. We don't know how long they had known one another. We don't know how long the man on the mat had been paralyzed or what caused his problem. We don't even know if the man they carried came willingly or they insisted despite his doubts or objections. What we do know is that they cared about their friend and wanted to see him get well. We know they believed in Jesus' power enough to carry their friend to Jesus.

In community, sometimes we are those who carry, and sometimes we are those who are carried. So let's consider both sides of the story.

Those Who Carry

Let's begin by talking about what it was like to be the friends who carried this man to Jesus. Their task was hard, heavy work. They had to find the right materials and route, communicate and balance with one another, and keep a pace all four could agree on and manage. If you've ever carried furniture with other people, imagine balancing a physically fragile person on the top of that furniture! But they cared enough about their friend to be inventive and resourceful. They were determined to get him help. They were so determined that when they arrived at the house Jesus was teaching in and found that the crowds extended outside the doors, they still looked for a way to get their friend in front of this healer. They loved him too much to give up.

> **We are much more comfortable being the ones who help others than needing help ourselves.**

When have you helped carry the burdens of someone else? How did it feel?

Unlike our shingled roofs, Capernaum roofs would have been much easier to dig through (see Extra Insight). Even so, imagine this group digging a hole big enough to lower a man through—and then coordinating their effort to lower him to the floor without dropping him! Their task wasn't easy, and it ended with a mess in someone's living room. But their love for their friend was greater than the obstacles in their path.

Reread Mark 2:5. When they finally got into the home and Jesus assessed the situation before Him, whose faith did Jesus notice?

It's beautiful to know that Jesus noticed the faith of those who brought their friend to Him. I'm sure there is someone in your life whose struggles weigh on your heart. Whether or not this person has faith in God, *you* do! You can bring your loved ones to Jesus in prayer, knowing that He hears your deep cries for them.

Those Who Are Carried

Now let's imagine what it was like to be the friend who was carried to Jesus. What would it be like to be unable to care for yourself? How would you react to friends who wanted to go to all lengths for you? What would you say when they hatched a crazy plan and began carrying you through the streets, making a spectacle that ended with climbing onto a house, digging through a roof, and lowering you to the floor inside? I can imagine myself saying things like, "Please, don't go to all this trouble just for me" or "Hey, you almost dropped me!" The man's emotions may have ranged from feeling insecure to annoyed to unworthy of such bold actions.

When have you needed others to step in and help with burdens that were greater than you could bear alone? How did it feel?

Being the person who needs help is not easy. Most of us would rather carry the mat than be carried. But we all need carrying sometimes. The Bible paints a picture of community where our burdens are not our own. They are to be shared

Capernaum homes were covered by beams that had branches and reeds over them, held together by dried mud. Homes often had an outside staircase leading up to the roof because it needed ongoing maintenance.[4]

> You can bring your loved ones to Jesus in prayer, knowing that He hears your deep cries for them.

with others when needed, but never in a way that is unhealthy or exempts us from personal responsibility.

Look up the following Scriptures about bearing one another's burdens, and note how each paints a picture of community:

Psalm 133:1

Luke 10:30-37

1 Corinthians 13:7

Hebrews 10:24-25

Galatians 6:1-10

Now look again at Galatians 6:2-5 (NIV), and fill in the blanks below:

"Carry each other's _____*."* (v. 2)

"For each one should carry their own _____*."* (v. 5)

Throughout the Scriptures we are reminded to carry one another's burdens. The Greek word for burden in Galatians 6:2 is *baros*, which means a weight or a heavy load, a boulder that is too heavy to carry alone.[5] If someone has a boulder to bear, they need help from the community around them. Then in verse 5, we're reminded that each should carry their own load. The word for load in Greek is *phortion*, which refers to an individual pack that one person would carry.[6] Think of this as a backpack. So we are meant to carry a backpack load by ourselves, not a boulder load.

Overload isn't good for any of us, and when we see someone struggling, we often are able to use the strength God has given us to come alongside the person and help. But we need to remember not to become enablers who pick up so many backpacks of others, which they could carry on their own, that the weight becomes a burden on us. In order to decide when to help and when to step back, we often have to pray and seek God's guidance as well as ask others for advice.

In order to decide when to help and when to step back, we often have to pray and seek God's guidance as well as ask others for advice.

Has there been a time when you were trying to carry too many "backpacks" for others? If so, how did you come to this realization, and what did you do about it?

Once the man was lowered to the ground of a now-messy house with a disassembled roof, Jesus surprised everyone by declaring, "Son, your sins are forgiven" (Mark 2:5). Remember, Jesus wants to heal the whole person—spiritual, physical, emotional, relational—so He started with the man's sins. The reaction around him was anything but positive.

Reread Mark 5:17. What did the Pharisees and teachers of the law who were present think about what Jesus said?

As religious experts, they knew only God could offer forgiveness, and in their religious system that was done through sacrifices made by the high priest at the temple. Jesus' statement seemed blasphemous to them, as if He was claiming to be God.

But Jesus wasn't done. He continued, healing the man's body as well as His soul. As evidence of this, He commanded the man to get up, pick up his mat, and walk. The man who had been carried in was now carrying his own burden out!

Reread Mark 2:12. How did the people respond?

We're told that everyone was amazed and praised God. *Everyone*. That means that the doubting and outraged Pharisees were also praising God in amazement! This miracle of healing pointed people to the truth about Jesus: He *was* the Son of God, able to heal bodies and forgive sins.

The group of friends had been right to bring their struggling friend here. They knew better than to believe they could fix their friend's problems themselves, but they knew that Jesus was the One who could.

Take a minute to think about your own community. What burdens can you take to God on behalf of your friends? List them below and spend a moment in prayer, interceding for your friends.

Now ask God for some ways you can bless and encourage people in your circle of friends. List those ideas below:

This is the role of Christian community: We share strength when we have it; we ask for help when we need it.

At times our burdens will outweigh our ability to carry them. We'll find ourselves desperate and need to depend on others or sink beneath the load. God paints a picture of community as a place of shared struggle and shared joy. This is the role of Christian community: We share strength when we have it; we ask for help when we need it. Sometimes we're on the mat; sometimes we carry it. But it's always right to bring our own needs, and those of our friends, to Jesus. He is the answer to every burden.

Talk with God

Lord, *give me the strength to help carry others' burdens when they need it and the grace to admit when I need to be carried. I bring You those whose struggles seem too great to bear right now, carrying them to You in prayer, and I ask You to make them whole. I lift up . . . (name specific individuals and needs). Amen.*

DAY 3: JESUS SPEAKS AND EVIL FLEES THE SCENE

Read God's Word

[14]*When they came to the other disciples, they saw a large crowd around them and the teachers of the law arguing with them.* [15]*As soon as all the people saw Jesus, they were overwhelmed with wonder and ran to greet him.*

[16]*"What are you arguing with them about?" he asked.*

[17]A man in the crowd answered, "Teacher, I brought you my son, who is possessed by a spirit that has robbed him of speech. [18]Whenever it seizes him, it throws him to the ground. He foams at the mouth, gnashes his teeth and becomes rigid. I asked your disciples to drive out the spirit, but they could not."

[19]"You unbelieving generation," Jesus replied, "how long shall I stay with you? How long shall I put up with you? Bring the boy to me."

[20]So they brought him. When the spirit saw Jesus, it immediately threw the boy into a convulsion. He fell to the ground and rolled around, foaming at the mouth.

[21]Jesus asked the boy's father, "How long has he been like this?"

"From childhood," he answered. [22]"It has often thrown him into fire or water to kill him. But if you can do anything, take pity on us and help us."

[23]"'If you can'?" said Jesus. "Everything is possible for one who believes."

[24]Immediately the boy's father exclaimed, "I do believe; help me overcome my unbelief!"

[25]When Jesus saw that a crowd was running to the scene, he rebuked the impure spirit. "You deaf and mute spirit," he said, "I command you, come out of him and never enter him again."

[26]The spirit shrieked, convulsed him violently and came out. The boy looked so much like a corpse that many said, "He's dead." [27]But Jesus took him by the hand and lifted him to his feet, and he stood up.

[28]After Jesus had gone indoors, his disciples asked him privately, "Why couldn't we drive it out?"

[29]He replied, "This kind can come out only by prayer."

(Mark 9:14-29 NIV)

Reflect and Respond

In our modern culture, we almost never use words such as *demons, possession,* and *exorcism.* Just typing those words on a laptop in the twenty-first century seems so strange. For some, those ideas may seem archaic in the age of science; for others, evil and the spiritual topics associated with it are much more a part of their vocabulary. Depending on the church traditions in which we've grown up (if any at all), the idea of Jesus freeing a little boy from demon possession can be challenging to understand and apply in our lives. Yet in today's healing story we find Jesus performing a miracle that can help us understand more about our God who heals. Together we will seek to understand what this miracle meant for this boy and his family as well as what it means for us today in our walk with God.

This miracle occurs in three of the four Gospels, and they share similar headings in my Bible:

Mark 9: Jesus H*eals* a Boy Possessed by an Impure Spirit

Matthew 17 and Luke 9: Jesus H*eals* a Demon-Possessed Boy

The headings placed before each section are, of course, not the inspired Word of God as are the other words in the Bible. They have been placed there by editors. But this particular editor, I believe, got something right: the word *heals*.

Healing is a big part of what Jesus was about in His ministry of restoring God's kingdom on earth, and releasing people from demons was one of the types of healing miracles that Jesus practiced. Today when we think of healing, we often focus on the symptoms of our physical bodies. But in Jesus' culture, there was no dividing line between a person's physical, spiritual, and emotional well-being. In many ways, we are rediscovering this today, as doctors and researchers are finding evidence that much of our emotional and physical health are bound up together.

Biblical passages about demon possession have sometimes been read by the church in ways that have been harmful to people who are suffering diseases such as epilepsy or mental illness. We should never assume that symptoms we can't understand or see a root cause for are necessarily rooted in spiritual causes. Jumping to conclusions that human symptoms have demonic roots can be damaging to the persons most affected. On the other hand, just because we cannot see, control, or even fully understand something does not mean that it's not real. The Bible often helps open our eyes to the unseen spiritual roots of visible realities.

In the culture in which Jesus lived and performed miracles, it was very common to speak about demons and being released from the power of demons through exorcism. Some interpret these texts as metaphors, talking about how we can be "freed from our demons" or our struggles. And there is certainly truth in the idea that our own struggles are sometimes our demons. But others believe that it's clear Jesus was talking here about, and even talking *to*, something or someone. We're often much more comfortable talking about the spiritual beings embodied in the good (angels) than we are wondering if there are opposite forces at work for evil as well.

Read Ephesians 6:10-12. What do these verses tell us about the forces that come in opposition to us?

Now read 1 Peter 5:8-9. What does Peter say we are struggling against, and what encouragement does he give us?

Extra Insight

In many cases healers in Jesus' day had elaborate rituals of magic or concoctions to treat the possessed person. This is why Jesus' ability to cast out spirits using only His words so amazed the people.

It was actually so commonplace in Jesus' day for people to talk about and witness the personification of evil in demons or "impure spirits" that their reactions to Jesus' miracles may seem a little ho-hum to us. In the first chapter of Mark's Gospel, Jesus frees a man from an unclean spirit, and it is a pretty confrontational and chaotic moment. Jesus shouts, "Be quiet! . . . Come out of him!" and then we read, "The impure spirit shook the man violently and came out of him with a shriek" (Mark 1:25-26 NIV).

Now, if this happened in the middle of a crowd today, people would be aghast. And the people watching Jesus were, too—but not why we might expect.

Read Mark 1:27-28 to find out what the people were most shocked by. What did they say "amazed" them before they ever referred to impure spirits?

Think about the significance of this. The amazement they expressed at Jesus' command over the spirit was secondary to the fact that Jesus had simply used words or commands to produce results—nothing more (see Extra Insight). This emphasized to the people Jesus' incredible power and authority over evil. His power can be displayed simply by speaking a word, as we've seen in other miracle stories.

Review the story of the calming of the storm found in Mark 4:35-41, which we've read previously (page 77). How did Jesus demonstrate His power?

Again and again in the Gospels, Jesus shows us God's desire to come to the rescue of His children—oftentimes with just a word.

The emphasis in this story of the demon-possessed boy is on *faith*. First, the boy's father complained to Jesus that the disciples had already tried to help his son and had failed. Jesus' response was to chastise the disciples for their lack of faith: "You unbelieving generation." And then He told the father, "Bring the boy to me" (Mark 9:19 NIV). The disciples had been trying to do this on their

Jesus shows us God's desire to come to the rescue of His children— oftentimes with just a word.

own, without relying on Jesus. And Jesus reminded them that He alone is the source of healing.

The way to help others is not in our own strength but to "bring them to Jesus," something we can do through prayer.

Have you ever tried to help someone in your own strength? If so, what happened?

Whom have you "brought to Jesus" in prayer recently?

What are some other ways we can bring people to Jesus for His healing touch?

The next part of the story that highlights faith is the moment when we clearly see how desperate the father was. Nothing brings someone to their knees like the desperate love of a parent for a child. It is both the most wonderful and most vulnerable kind of love there is.

Jesus responded to the father's request by saying, "Everything is possible for one who believes" (Mark 9:23 NIV), and the father reacted with what is, for me, one of the most cherished phrases in all of Scripture.

Reread Mark 9:24, and write the father's response below:

We are a people who have faith and need faith all at once.

The father expressed a desire to believe wholeheartedly in Jesus while at the same time he confessed a cautious, tentative hope. He had faith, but he lacked faith. If we're honest, most of us in our greatest moments of need could say the same thing to God. We are a people who have faith and need faith all at once.

When has this been true in your own life? When could you cry out to Jesus, "I do believe" while at the same time beg, "Help me overcome my unbelief"?

What were you sure of at this time?

What did you need help to believe at this time?

We can easily slip into the fear that without *perfect* faith, our cries for God's help will be ignored. But praise God, Jesus' response of healing this little boy shows us this isn't the case! This story tells us that Jesus' powerful response to our needs isn't a result of our own piety or certainty; it is because of the grace of God Himself.

At the end of this miracle story, the disciples asked Jesus where they went wrong.

Review Mark 9:29. What did Jesus say this kind of miracle required?

Theologian Dr. Ben Witherington puts it this way:

Jesus informs them that they have failed because this type of exorcism requires prayer, which is to say constant reliance on the source of power! The power is conveyed through communion with the Almighty; it is not inherently resident in the disciples on an ongoing basis without such communion.[7]

In other words, prayer is the power source for God's miraculous work in our lives. When we feel a lack of power or faith, we can lean into our source of power found through our communion with God in prayer. Evil is real; that's certain to anyone who's paying attention in life. But Jesus is more powerful than evil. More powerful than sickness. More powerful than death. He has the power to heal us—physically, spiritually, and emotionally—and He has ultimate victory over all evil. That's something we can be certain of!

Talk with God

Loving God, I confess that often I lack belief. Help me to lean into communion with You so that I can believe and experience the power that only You can provide—power to push back the darkness and speak words of healing to those around me. Teach me what I need to know about who You are and how You want to work in my life. Amen.

> Jesus' powerful response to our needs isn't a result of our own piety or certainty; it is because of the grace of God Himself.

> When we feel a lack of power or faith, we can lean into our source of power found through our communion with God in prayer.

DAY 4: NO SECOND-CLASS PRAY-ERS

Read God's Word

²⁴[Jesus] *set out and went away to the region of Tyre. He entered a house and did not want anyone to know he was there. Yet he could not escape notice,* ²⁵*but a woman whose little daughter had an unclean spirit immediately heard about him, and she came and bowed down at his feet.* ²⁶*Now the woman was a Gentile, of Syrophoenician origin. She begged him to cast the demon out of her daughter.* ²⁷*He said to her, "Let the children be fed first, for it is not fair to take the children's food and throw it to the dogs."* ²⁸*But she answered him, "Sir, even the dogs under the table eat the children's crumbs."* ²⁹*Then he said to her, "For saying that, you may go—the demon has left your daughter."* ³⁰*So she went home, found the child lying on the bed, and the demon gone.*

(Mark 7:24-30)

Reflect and Respond

When I spotted the event announcement in a magazine highlighting classes for local writers, it was as if they had created an event just for me:

All night Write-In – 8:00 p.m. to 8:00 a.m.

Join a group of local writers overnight for writing sprints, fellowship, and guaranteed progress on your current project. Pizza, snacks, and breakfast provided.

As a lifelong night owl and pizza lover, I knew I had to attend! At three in the morning, though, bleary-eyed and jittery from too much coffee, I was wondering if this was such a great idea. My progress had started off at 8:00 p.m. with a rushing river of ideas and slowed to a babbling brook around 11:00 p.m.; now here it was 3:00 a.m. and there was not even a trickle.

During a break, a similarly groggy group began gathering near the coffee, waiting for a fresh pot to brew. As we got to know one another, people began sharing what they were writing. An older woman was writing mysteries while her friend who came with her was writing poetry. A seventeen-year-old girl kept glancing at her phone: she had convinced her parents to let her stay past her curfew, promising that she would finish college essays when she really wanted to write short stories. A twenty-something man in an orange T-shirt and saggy jeans said he was working on a dystopian novel. Then suddenly they were all looking at me.

"Miracles," I blurted out. "I'm writing a book about miracles and how our desperation is actually a good thing because it's what comes before a miracle."

Since writers are a pretty unusual crew anyway, they didn't bat an eye at the odd subject matter. But one of the older women spoke up, saying matter-of-factly, "Except they don't happen to us. You can pray for a miracle all you want, but no one is really listening." I wondered for the rest of the night about that woman, wishing I knew what her story was and what unwritten miracle she had been waiting for that hadn't happened.

One of the most difficult issues to address when talking about miracles, especially healing miracles, is the question of unanswered prayer. Many of us have prayed—or are currently praying—for healings that didn't happen. It can cause us to doubt God, to doubt ourselves, to become angry or jealous, and to feel forgotten.

But as we'll be reminded in our study today, our lives and the cries of our hearts matter to God. He tells us that He knows us *intimately*.

Read Luke 12:7 in the margin. What does this verse tell us about God's love and care for us?

"Even the hairs of your head are all counted. Do not be afraid; you are of more value than many sparrows."

(Luke 12:7)

God knows the number of hairs on our heads, and although He pays attention to the tiniest of birds, we are worth more than a whole flock of them! When you wonder if God sees you, hears you, and cares about you and your concerns, remember that it's just not possible for God to forget about you.

Read Isaiah 49:14-16. How does God answer a people who wonder if God has forgotten them? What metaphors does He use to describe how He feels about them and how present their names and identities are to Him?

While the details of our hearts' most intimate cries are important to God, our perspective on His eternal story must always be bigger than the rise or fall of one set of circumstances. I want to encourage you to keep three things in mind when prayers go unanswered.

1. Don't assume you are a second-class citizen.

Sometimes when prayers go unanswered, we may feel like second-class citizens in the kingdom of God, as if God has heard and cared about the

When you wonder if God sees you, hears you, and cares about you and your concerns, remember that it's just not possible for God to forget about you.

concerns of others but forgotten about us. I know when my own prayers have lingered in the unanswered column I've wondered if God was really listening, or if there was some reason He was withholding the blessings I considered so easy to bestow.

If anyone could have felt like a second-class citizen in Jesus' presence, it would have been the Syrophoenician woman. It's unfortunate that we don't know her name, but we're reminded of a central point about her every time we call her "the Syrophoenician woman." Mark tells us in his Gospel, "The woman was a Gentile, of Syrophoenician origin" (Mark 7:26). This description tells us that she was not Jewish, which meant that she was an outsider to the Jewish faith. Being Jew or Greek was a dividing line among the people in that culture, and Jews often looked down on people outside the faith as those undeserving of God's blessings. A common misconception among the Jews was that their status as "God's chosen people" meant that God would bless them but not others.

Read Genesis 12:1-2 in the margin. What did God tell Abram and Sarai was the purpose of their blessings? Whom would God use them to bless?

The Jews in Jesus' day did not expect much faith from pagan outsiders, especially from a pagan woman such as this one.[8] And they would have remembered that the most prominent woman from Phoenicia, which was the same region where the Syrophoenician woman was from, was the wicked Jezebel. So, it must have been surprising when this woman dared to come inside a house where Jesus was staying and approach Him boldly, falling at His feet and asking Him to heal her daughter from demon possession. Those gathered around might have been shocked that she would dare come to Jesus at all—and perhaps even more shocked by His response.

Before we get to Jesus' response, let's take a step back and look at the full chapter of Mark 7 where this story is found in order to find a clue about why Jesus responded to her as He did. In the previous verses in this chapter, Jesus had a conversation with the Pharisees about things that would make a person spiritually clean—able to come into worship and into contact with God with a pure heart—or unclean. While the Pharisees were arguing that the most important thing in maintaining purity before God was washing hands in a certain way before eating or avoiding certain foods because they were clean or unclean, Jesus had other ideas.

¹The Lord said to Abram, "Go from your country and your kindred and your father's house to the land that I will show you. ²I will make of you a great nation, and I will bless you, and make your name great, so that you will be a blessing.

(Genesis 12:1-2)

Read Mark 7:14-15 in the margin. What did Jesus declare to the crowd that He called around Him?

14He called the crowd again and said to them, "Listen to me, all of you, and understand: 15there is nothing outside a person that by going in can defile, but the things that come out are what defile."

(Mark 7:14-15)

Jesus went on to shock the crowd He had called around Him by telling them there were no longer any unclean foods for Jews since what is in people's hearts is the true indicator of righteousness, not what is in their stomachs (Mark 7:18-23). It was immediately after this conversation with the Pharisees that Jesus encountered the woman from Syrophoenicia (Mark 7:24-30). And immediately after His conversation with her, as He was traveling through a region called Sidon, Jesus healed a non-Jewish man who was deaf and mute (Mark 7:31-37). These stories are a three-part package in which Jesus loudly proclaims that God's creation—the food He has made and especially the people He has made—are good in God's eyes.

So, with this insight, let's return to the unusual exchange between Jesus and the woman when she asked Him for healing for her daughter.

Reread Mark 7:27. What did Jesus say to her?

This comment has puzzled many and made them wonder if Jesus was dishonoring the woman by referring to her in this way. Yet we need to remember that Jesus was referring to the Jews as "children" in the same way that Exodus 4:22 says, "Israel is my firstborn son." As we read previously in Genesis 12:1-2, God blessed Israel so that through them He could bless other nations and thus the entire world.

Read John 4:22 in the margin. Where does salvation for the world come from?

"You worship what you do not know; we worship what we know, for salvation is from the Jews."

(John 4:22)

Jesus was reiterating the idea of Israel being the firstborn in the family of God; however, that relationship was for the sake of saving the *whole world*. All of those God has made are good in His eyes. God has no second-class citizens!

Have you ever felt that you are a second-class citizen in God's kingdom? If so, what do you think has contributed to this feeling?

What encouragement and reassurance do you find in these three stories in Mark 7?

Remember that no matter if your prayers fall into the answered or unanswered column, you are precious to God! He made you, He loves you, and He is always listening and longing for relationship with you.

2. Don't stop praying.

When our prayers go unanswered, we also can be tempted to quit praying. *After all, what's the point?* we may wonder. But we can learn a lesson in persistence from the Syrophoenician woman.

Reread Mark 7:28. What did the woman say in response to Jesus?

Rather than give up and walk away, she noted that even the lowliest member of the family deserves to be fed. This comment is evidence of her determination and persistence before God. Her request for a small crumb of Jesus' mercy indicates that she believed even the smallest fraction of Jesus' power would heal her daughter. This was a big vision of God for a woman who had been shut out of the community of faith. And we know from other miracles what Jesus can do with the smallest of crumbs!

Recall a time when you persisted in prayer for some time. What were you praying for? How did God respond to your prayers?

Is there a persistent prayer you are still waiting for God to answer? If so, what is it?

If answers to your prayers seem far off, don't back away from God. Lean in. Keep praying with bold humility. In Scripture, blessings often come to those who will not give up in their pursuit of God.

Look up the following Old Testament passages that demonstrate faith expressed in bold zeal, and note how boldness or even desperation was demonstrated.

By women of faith in 2 Kings 4:14-28

By prophets in Exodus 33:12–34:9; 1 Kings 18:36-37; and 2 Kings 2:2, 4, 6, 9

By other heroes in Genesis 32:26-30

As one source notes, all of these examples "combine humble respect for God or his prophet with boldly urgent entreaty, and God answers these prayers."[9] So the Syrophoenician woman is in good company by continuing her request—and then receiving a blessing from God.

Take another look at Mark 7:29-30. What was the result of the woman's persistent faith?

According to the Gospel of Mark, Jesus won every controversial conversation He had with the religious authorities, yet He allowed Himself to be persuaded by this desperate parent. Take that in for a moment. Desperate persistence moves the heart of God! This story encourages us to keep asking, knocking, and persisting in prayer when it seems that our petitions are not being answered. Though we may not get the outcome we've asked for in prayer, we can always count on being blessed in response to our persistent faith.

3. Don't forget God's view is bigger than ours.

A third thing that can happen when prayers go unanswered is that we can develop tunnel vision. We can become so focused on our unmet requests that we fail to see the bigger picture of all God is doing in and around us. As we persist and seek God in prayer, we must keep in mind that our human view is so much smaller and more limited than God's all-encompassing and eternal view.

> Though we may not get the outcome we've asked for in prayer, we can always count on being blessed in response to our persistent faith.

> **As we persist and seek God in prayer, we must keep in mind that our human view is so much smaller and more limited than God's all-encompassing and eternal view.**

Imagine the prayers the disciples prayed on Good Friday as Jesus was beaten, condemned, and then executed on the cross. Don't you imagine that every single one of them prayed for things to go differently? And was anyone ever as deserving of those prayers being answered as Jesus was? In their short view of the situation, the disciples' prayers went unanswered. But then came Easter! God had a longer view, a plan that would change their lives and the entire world forever.

What are some of your struggles with unanswered prayer? How have you responded to these struggles?

What would you tell someone who is struggling with unanswered prayer?

If we pray long enough, it's highly likely that we all will have prayers that remain unanswered. But even the act of persistent prayer leads us to the source of comfort, mercy, and truth. Our prayers may not always elicit the exact response we're longing for, but they always end in a connection with Christ. When we make the effort to pray, we know that God hears and that our prayers, even when they're full of frustration and anger, are beautiful in God's ears. Jesus' compassionate response to a persistent woman who was an outsider shows us that He is listening and hears our cries.

We can know with confidence that we are loved and heard by God!

Unanswered prayer and unreceived blessings are some of the hardest hurdles that those of us who follow Jesus deal with. But the best place for us to be when we are hurting or uncertain or even angry is in God's presence. Whether or not your prayers lead to the answer your heart longs for, they lead you to Jesus, which is what His heart longs for! Don't give up praying, and know that God will never give up listening.

Talk with God

Lord, I know I'm not alone in questioning why You heal some and not others. Give me faith to believe that when prayers go unanswered, You still hold everything together in Your loving hands. When I am desperate, compel me to lean into You. Give me faith to pray and ask from You what only You can give. Amen.

DAY 5: DO YOU WANT TO BE MADE WELL?

Read God's Word

¹After this there was a festival of the Jews, and Jesus went up to Jerusalem.

²Now in Jerusalem by the Sheep Gate there is a pool, called in Hebrew Beth-zatha, which has five porticoes. ³In these lay many invalids—blind, lame, and paralyzed.* ⁵One man was there who had been ill for thirty-eight years. ⁶When Jesus saw him lying there and knew that he had been there a long time, he said to him, "Do you want to be made well?" ⁷The sick man answered him, "Sir, I have no one to put me into the pool when the water is stirred up; and while I am making my way, someone else steps down ahead of me." ⁸Jesus said to him, "Stand up, take your mat and walk." ⁹At once the man was made well, and he took up his mat and began to walk.

Now that day was a sabbath. ¹⁰So the Jews said to the man who had been cured, "It is the sabbath; it is not lawful for you to carry your mat." ¹¹But he answered them, "The man who made me well said to me, 'Take up your mat and walk.'" ¹²They asked him, "Who is the man who said to you, 'Take it up and walk'?" ¹³Now the man who had been healed did not know who it was, for Jesus had disappeared in the crowd that was there. ¹⁴Later Jesus found him in the temple and said to him, "See, you have been made well! Do not sin any more, so that nothing worse happens to you." ¹⁵The man went away and told the Jews that it was Jesus who had made him well.

(John 5:1-15)

Reflect and Respond

In 1996, a zoo in Copenhagen put a new kind of animal on display in its primate exhibit: a pair of homo sapiens. The exhibit was inhabited by a man and woman—Henrik Lehmann, an acrobat, and Malene Botoft, a newspaper employee—who said their purpose was to help visitors think about their origins and relationship to the animals in nature.

Their 320-square-foot habitat included a living room with furniture, a computer, a television, and stereo and was attached to a kitchen and bedroom also on display. Only the bathroom (thankfully) was hidden from public view. The couple did what humans do every day: resting, watching TV, eating, and working—except there was a steady stream of strangers shuffling past to stare at them through glass.

Unlike their primate neighbors, their door was unlocked. They had the freedom to wander out when they needed to shop, visit friends, or run home to

* Critical editions of the early Greek New Testament manuscripts do not include a portion of the text that ends verse 3 nor do they include verse 4.

water the plants; but they did so less and less, becoming so comfortable with the walls around them that they chose to mostly stay inside and even began to forget the confinement and restrictive limitations of the enclosure around them.[10]

It's both a gift and a curse of human nature that we can adapt to the conditions we find ourselves in. But when those conditions are less than the freedom God intended for us, sometimes we can become so complacent in our captivity that we forget there is more. We can actually miss the healing God wants to do in our lives because we've become complacent with our status quo. Thankfully, God isn't ever complacent or satisfied with less than the full dream He had for us in Creation from the beginning. He is always busy drawing us out into the bigger world from the walls we've become used to, bringing restoration and wholeness.

The man in this story from the Gospel of John had been sick his entire life. His sickness had a lifespan longer than many people even lived in the first century—thirty-eight years. He was alone, with no family to assist or comfort him. He spent his days gathered with other sick people around a pool they thought was their only hope for healing. Their lives were defined by illness: the blind, lame, and crippled, all hoping for healing. They weren't well enough to work or pure enough to go to the temple, so their illness created its own kind of community for them. The pools themselves were the reason they gathered there: a superstition held that whoever got in the pool first when the waters were stirred or bubbling would be healed. But with such a backlog of the sick, it's unlikely their desires for magical healing were placed in something worthy of that kind of hope.

When Jesus stood over the lame man, perhaps blocking his view of the pool that held his hopes for healing and the community that held his identity in sickness, it was a moment completely unexpected. The man hadn't seen Jesus or called him over, but for some reason Jesus singled him out among all those gathered. Then Jesus asked an unexpected question.

Write the question Jesus asked the man in John 5:6 here:

How did the man answer Jesus in verse 7?

What kind of question was that for someone who had been sick longer than most people in his generation had been alive? *Do you want to get well?* This man probably had prayed more prayers than we can imagine and had sought every kind of help that was available to him, including putting his faith

Extra Insight

The twin pools at Beth-zatha (or Bethesda) were each as large as a football field and about twenty feet deep, with covered porches all around and one running down the center between the two.[11] The sick and lame would lie beneath these porches.

in this bubbling water. Surely there had been enough desperation to call for ten miracles!

But it's not always a given that we want to get well. Jesus knows to ask because unless we are partners in our own healing by relying more on Jesus than we have on the limited world in which we've lived in the past, we will return to captivity—whether it's the same or another kind.

Do you want to be made well? The question reminds us that sometimes our brokenness—becomes home to us, making the hardship of the past seem safer than the unknowns of freedom that lie ahead. What would it mean for this man to be made well? He'd have to be responsible for his life now, to invest fully in relationships instead of being passively cared for, to work for his food, and to participate fully in the world. His broken state, as hard as it had been, may have seemed to be a comfortable, known world of safety—and less risky than a new and unknown life outside the walls of sickness.

Have you ever known someone who seemed so comfortable in his or her brokenness that the person wasn't willing to "be made well"? If so, describe the situation:

Have you ever thought that it would be safer to stay the same instead of letting Jesus change you, even if it would be for the better? If so, what happened?

The Gospel of John tells us that this healing happened on the Sabbath. This is an important detail, so let's unpack it a bit.

The Sabbath is a day of rest given to us as a gift from God. God rested on the seventh day of Creation not because He was tired—after all, an all-powerful God can't be tired—but because He wanted to model for His people what completion or wholeness looks like. When Creation was complete or whole, God stepped back and sanctified it with a day that was set apart from the others.

So, one reason for Sabbath rest is to recognize God's sovereignty over creation—which includes you and me—as the Creator. Later when God's people were reminded to keep the Sabbath, it was a way for them to remember this. Even today, when we are tempted to find our identity in our work or our hurried lifestyles, Sabbath reminds us that we are so much more in God's eyes: we are His beloved creations.

> Sometimes our brokenness becomes home to us, making the hardship of the past seem safer than the unknowns of freedom that lie ahead.

> When we are tempted to find our identity in our work or our hurried lifestyles, Sabbath reminds us that, in God's eyes, we are so much more.

A second reason for Sabbath rest was to commemorate the Exodus, when God freed His people from the bondage of slavery in Egypt. When God's people were slaves, they could not take a day to rest or worship. Now a day of rest for all households—including servants—would remind them that they had been freed from tyranny and should model God's loving-kindness to others.

Even though Sabbath was a gift meant to provide rest and assurance of God's love, over time God's people made it a rule rather than a celebration. In fact, they made rules about how to follow the rules! Instead of finding joy and peace in the Sabbath, God's people often associated it with fear and legalism as they tried to decide exactly what the rule of Sabbath prohibited them from doing.

When Jesus healed on the Sabbath, the rule-enforcing Pharisees found themselves in a dilemma. On one hand, they observed Jesus doing "work," which was prohibited. On the other hand, the healings that the crowds witnessed on these Sabbath days were clearly acts of the kind of *shalom* (peace) and wholeness that were compatible with God's original vision for Sabbath.

Look up three or more of these healings that Jesus performed on the Sabbath. What are some of the things Jesus healed people from on the Sabbath?

Mark 1:21-28   _____

Luke 4:38-39   _____

Mark 3:1-6   _____

Luke 13:10-17   _____

Luke 14:1-6   _____

John 9:1-34   _____

What did we say are two reasons for Sabbath rest? What does it embody? Look back for the answers and write them below:

_____

_____

Sabbath is a vision of wholeness and restoration, and Jesus beautifully embodied that vision when He healed people on the Sabbath. His healings celebrated God's recreating of His world by healing the broken and making all things new. His healings also broke the bondage of sickness and death and restored freedom to those who received healing.

Look again at John 5:8-9. What did Jesus tell the man to do? What happened next?

When this lame man was healed, Jesus commanded him to get up, carry his mat, and walk. The Jewish leaders—those who were very invested in making and enforcing rules about how to keep the Sabbath—found that the man was walking around with his mat, and they were upset.

Read the Scriptures below, and note what each warns against:

Numbers 15:32-35

Jeremiah 17:21

Clearly it was against the law to carry burdens on the Sabbath, and so carrying a mat could be interpreted as work.

What did the religious leaders say to the man in John 5:10?

Jesus' act of healing on the Sabbath, which embodied God's grace and love, stands in stark contrast to the religious leaders' concerns about doing work on the Sabbath—evidence of their cold and rigid practice of religion. Jesus lifted the man's burden of sickness and commanded him to pick up the very thing he had laid on all of his life in despair. The Jewish teachers were offended to find him carrying his mat, showing that they cared more about rules than about the man's healing. Their way of seeing God's law only burdened the man, while Jesus' gift of healing set him free.

Now look again at John 5:12-13. What question did they ask the man, and how did he answer?

Isn't that great? When they asked the man who had given him this law-breaking command to carry his mat, he didn't even know Jesus' identity! I love the idea that people can be touched by God before they even realize who God is. The man had one more chance to learn who Jesus was when he later met Him in the temple. Jesus' words of greeting may seem strange to us.

Reread John 5:14. What did Jesus tell the man?

It's interesting how often Jesus connected physical healing with references to the problem of sin and freedom from sin. Jesus was not saying that the man's sin had caused his sickness; rather, He recognized that as burdened as the man had been from physical problems, the sin in his life would burden him even more if he did not find a new way of living for God. Sin can cause something worse than physical illness because it can be spiritually fatal. Jesus wanted this man to be healed and whole in body *and* spirit, and He wouldn't stop "stirring up" the waters of his life until the man was restored to the way God intended in Creation.

How has God been speaking to you as we've studied healing this week? I hope you've heard the message again and again that Jesus wants nothing but the best for you—nothing short of your wholeness and restoration. God's goal is the complete restoration and wholeness of His creation, of which you are a treasured part! Know that Jesus' desire for your complete wholeness is a part of a grander picture that will restore the world to the beauty and completeness of Eden. He loves you and the rest of creation so much that nothing will stand in His way! May God bless you as you seek the healing and wholeness that can come only from Him.

Talk with God

Lord, like the man beside the pool, I want to be made well. You are a great healer and deliverer. Thank You that You are for me and want me to be whole and well. Please take away anything that stands in the way of my restoration. I am desperate for You. Come and do what only You can do. Amen.

VIDEO VIEWER GUIDE: WEEK 4

Mark 8:22-25

Healing or wholeness lies in admitting that you need _____.

God's work is ___*slow*___ —even ___*imperceptable*___ sometimes.

The most ___*blind*___ people are often the ones who proclaim to ___*follow*___ Jesus.

Our darkness is revealed most by how we ___*see*___ and ___*treat*___ the people around us.

Ephesians 4:16

It's our ___*difficulties*___ in relationships that often reveal our blindness, and it's our ___*participation*___ in relationships that often brings our second-touch cure.

Week 5

A TWO-FOR-ONE
MIRACLE STORY

The Power of True Love

...rk 5:21-43 all this week, the verses have been
...e overlap). However, there will be times when
...ad or back in your workbook to read another
...pen your Bible to Mark 5 each day and read

...boat to the other side, a great crowd gathered
...Then one of the leaders of the synagogue named
... at his feet ²³*and begged him repeatedly, "My*
...Come and lay your hands on her, so that she
...ent with him.

...ssed in on him. ²⁵*Now there was a woman*
... hemorrhages for twelve years. ²⁶*She had endured much
under many physicians, and had spent all that she had; and she was no better, but
rather grew worse.* ²⁷*She had heard about Jesus, and came up behind him in the crowd
and touched his cloak,* ²⁸*for she said, "If I but touch his clothes, I will be made well."*
²⁹*Immediately her hemorrhage stopped; and she felt in her body that she was healed
of her disease.* ³⁰*Immediately aware that power had gone forth from him, Jesus turned
about in the crowd and said, "Who touched my clothes?"* ³¹*And his disciples said to
him, "You see the crowd pressing in on you; how can you say, 'Who touched me?'"*
³²*He looked all around to see who had done it.* ³³*But the woman, knowing what had
happened to her, came in fear and trembling, fell down before him, and told him the
whole truth.* ³⁴*He said to her, "Daughter, your faith has made you well; go in peace, and
be healed of your disease."*

(Mark 5:21-34)

Reflect and Respond

Last week we explored five healing miracles of Jesus that show us God's heart
and purpose for restoration and wholeness when it comes to healing. We saw
that Jesus' goal for us is always more than a physical cure; it's nothing short of
full restoration in community with others and with God Himself. The process
we used was a little like window shopping, walking through the Gospels and
stopping to examine first one healing and then another on the rack. This week
we're going to spend an entire week on one healing story, but it's really a two-for-
one special! (And who doesn't love a BOGO, right?) Two healings happen within

one story, and the relationship between these two healings and the reasons they are paired in the Gospel of Mark are not only fascinating; they actually reveal the message in all of God's miracles: *God longs to show us His true and perfect love.*

These two miracles for the price of one occur in chapter 5 of the Gospel of Mark. Jesus is in the midst of a large crowd that is pressing in around Him when a religious leader named Jairus rushes in to beg for Jesus' help. His daughter is sick and dying. As Jesus is on His way to help, a woman who is very sick reaches out and touches His cloak in order to seek healing. These two events don't seem to be connected. Jairus does not know the woman and has never had any contact with her. But these two stories tell us even more together than they would have separately.[1] Let's look together first at their similarities, and tomorrow we will consider their differences.

The time-frame

Even if you are familiar with these two stories in Mark 5, it's likely that you have never noticed or paid much attention to this particular similarity. But as it turns out, this small detail is anything but insignificant.

Reread Mark 5:25. How long had the woman been ill?

Now read Mark 5:42 (Day 3, page 147). How old was the little girl?

The age of Jairus's daughter and the length of the woman's illness were the same: twelve years. This small detail is actually a major connection between the two stories. The severity of the woman's condition is made even clearer by the fact that she has been ill for as long as the little girl has been alive! Also remember that Israel was organized into twelve tribes descended from the twelve sons of Jacob (Ezekiel 47:13), and that Jesus' followers mirrored that number as twelve disciples. The connection in these healing stories to the twelve tribes and the twelve disciples reminds us of Jesus' desire to heal not only individual bodies but also the people of God as a corporate body. God loves us individually and listens to the cries of our hearts, but He's also looking with a focus on a bigger picture than we could ever imagine, gathering a people to Himself and working on the restoration of all of creation.

The threat of death

Another similarity we see in both stories is the threat of death. The first thing we learn from Jairus is the seriousness of his daughter's condition.

In Mark 5:23, what does Jairus tell Jesus, and what does he ask Jesus to do?

What clues do you find in Mark 5:25-26 that suggest the seriousness of the woman's condition?

Clearly Jairus's little girl is dying, and he is desperate to get Jesus to her before death claims her as a victim. Similarly, the condition of the bleeding woman is certainly leading her on a trajectory toward death. She has lost blood continually for twelve long years, and nothing she has tried has stopped the bleeding. The Old Testament emphasizes again and again the nature of blood as the "life fluid" of a living being.

Look up Leviticus 17:11 (NIV), and fill in the blanks below:

For the _____ *of a creature is in the*

_____.

Anyone who heard about this woman's plight with continual bleeding would have associated her story with death. It was only a matter of time before her life would be drained from her body through the loss of her blood. Both she and Jairus were fighting for life, and Jesus was the only One who could help them.

Has a sense of urgency ever compelled you to plead with Jesus? If so, write about it below:

The presence of noise, chaos, and commotion

Another common denominator of these two stories is the commotion in which they take place.

Look again at Mark 5:21 and 24. What pressed in around Jesus in both places?

This is what the LORD of
the Heavenly Armies says:

"Think about what
I'm saying!
Indeed, call out
the professional
mourners!
Send for the best
of them to come."
(Jeremiah 9:17 ISV)

———————————————

Therefore, this is what
the Lord, the LORD God of
Heaven's Armies, says:

"There will be crying in
all the public squares
and mourning in
every street.
Call for the farmers to
weep with you,
and summon
professional
mourners to wail.
(Amos 5:16 NLT)

Extra Insight

Because a group of
loud mourners was
already present in
Jairus's home when
Jesus arrived, this is
further indication
that the child had
indeed died.

Where there is a crowd, you can be sure there is commotion! Not only is there a noisy, turbulent crowd surrounding Jesus when both Jairus and the bleeding woman approach Him, but there also is a crowd waiting at Jairus's house.

Read Mark 5:35-37 (Day 2, page 147). What news do the people who come from the house of Jairus bring? (v. 35)

Read Mark 5:38 (Day 3, page 153). How does Mark describe the scene at Jairus's house? What are the people doing? (v. 38)

When Jesus finally arrives at Jairus's home, there is quite a commotion. A crowd of mourners has gathered, and there is loud crying and wailing. It's possible that these mourners were not even family or friends.

Read Jeremiah 9:17 and Amos 5:16 in the margin. What do both of these verses call for?

It was the custom in both Old and New Testament days for professional mourners to be hired by the family to make much noise, signaling a death to the community and also showing how loved the deceased was. So from beginning to end of both stories, we find noise, chaos, and commotion.

The presence of fear

Another commonality between the stories of Jairus and the bleeding woman is fear, which we see in their postures before Jesus.

Reread Mark 5:22-23. What is Jairus's posture before Jesus? How does he make his request?

Now look again at Mark 5:33. What is the woman's posture before Jesus in this moment? What do you imagine she is thinking and feeling?

Within a few verses of each other, both of these figures are kneeling before Jesus. We read that Jairus "begged him repeatedly"—which suggests the desperation caused by anxiety and fear. As a parent, I can only imagine how desperate he must have felt. It's intriguing that while he is afraid on the front end of his miracle, the bleeding woman's fear is mentioned after she is healed—at the discovery of what she has done.

Jesus calms the fear present in both of them with His actions and His words. He says to the woman, "Go in peace" (v. 34), and to Jairus, "Do not fear, only believe" (v. 36). Jesus' presence always overwhelms and extinguishes the presence of fear.

> Read Lamentations 3:57 and Isaiah 41:10 in the margin. What do you learn about God's approach to casting out fear from these verses?

When and how has God's presence helped calm your fears?

The presence of faith

Just as we see the presence of fear in both stories, so we see the presence of faith. It took great faith for the woman to approach Jesus—even to sneak up on Him for a secret healing.

> What does Jesus say about her faith in Mark 5:34?

It also took faith for Jairus, a leader in the religious community, to come to Jesus so publicly with his needs—and even more faith to continue to trust Jesus after he found out that his daughter had died.

Jesus' presence always overwhelms and extinguishes the presence of fear.

You came near when I called you,
and you said,
"Do not fear."
(Lamentations 3:57 NIV)

So do not fear, for I am with you;
do not be dismayed,
for I am your God.
I will strengthen you and help you;
I will uphold you
with my righteous
right hand.
(Isaiah 41:10 NIV)

Read Mark 5:36 (Day 2, page 141). How did Jesus encourage Jairus? What did Jesus tell him to do?

Both of these individuals lived with faith and fear at the same time. They remind us that sometimes we will feel both at once. Jesus doesn't need us to overcome fear on our own; He wants us to bring what little faith we have to Him so that He can help us with our fears.

"Immediately"

These two stories also share an important word.

Read verses 29 and 42 in the margin, and circle the word used in each to tell how quickly the healings occurred.

When Jesus reaches out to heal these two individuals, there is no delay. While not all of our needs or requests are remedied immediately, the use of this word in these stories emphasizes Jesus' power to heal.

Immediately her hemorrhage stopped; and she felt in her body that she was healed of her disease.

(Mark 5:29)

And immediately the girl got up and began to walk about

(Mark 5:42)

The return of peace and calm

Even in the midst of the chaotic crowd, Jesus calmly seeks to give His attention to one inconspicuous woman. As we've already seen, he tells her to "go in peace" (v. 34), a state very different from the way she entered the scene. Jesus is reassuring her that she has done nothing wrong in seeking healing and that He graciously gives what she has taken from Him.

Later when Jesus reaches Jairus's house, He drives the noisy mourners away before He goes to encounter the little girl (v. 40). When He brings their cherished daughter back to life, it restores peace and joy to the household.

These two human beings, the religious leader Jairus and the woman with a bleeding disorder, really had nothing in common (more on that tomorrow). If they had met on the street on an average day, they wouldn't have spoken to each other. It's likely they wouldn't even have walked down the same street! But they are united by these common experiences of suffering, fear, and desperation before Jesus. Their stories are also united by the overwhelming ability of Jesus to heal and restore, respond to their needs with compassion and grace, and change their world in a heartbeat.

Where is there noise and commotion, fear and anxiety, or sickness and mourning in your life right now?

How can you notice Jesus and reach out to Him even in the midst of it?

What encouragement have you found from what you've studied today?

If you've been through times of deep mourning, unrelenting sickness, heartbreaking love for a child, great concern for a loved one in desperate need, or simply times of commotion and chaos that seem to crowd out Jesus, then you are all too familiar with the anxiety, fear, and desperation in the stories we've explored today. My prayer for you is that the similar experiences of Jesus' compassion in these stories has a familiar ring to you as well. When you kneel before Him in need, may you see the look of immediate compassion and love in His eyes, and may chaos slip away in His comforting, peaceful presence.

Talk with God

Healing God, thank You for stopping in the middle of chaos to meet my needs. And thank You for this witness of Your compassion and kindness. Give me a boldness to run to You when I am desperate. When I am afraid, God, speak peace against my fears. I love You, Lord. Amen.

DAY 2: "DAUGHTER"

Read God's Word

[33] But the woman, knowing what had happened to her, came in fear and trembling, fell down before him, and told him the whole truth. [34] He said to her, "Daughter, your faith has made you well; go in peace, and be healed of your disease."

[35] While he was still speaking, some people came from the leader's house to say, "Your daughter is dead. Why trouble the teacher any further?" [36] But overhearing what they said, Jesus said to the leader of the synagogue, "Do not fear, only believe." [37] He allowed no one to follow him except Peter, James, and John, the brother of James.

(Mark 5:33-37)

Reflect and Respond

Yesterday we reflected on similarities in the two-for-one miracle story about the healing of Jairus's daughter and the bleeding woman. Today we'll look at

some differences in their encounters with Jesus and what we can learn from His responses to each of them. Despite the differences in these individuals and their situations, both have something in common: an encounter with Jesus' compassionate, unfailing love.

Since we are introduced to Jairus first at the beginning of the story, let's begin with him. Jairus is a named leader in the synagogue, a man of power and privilege with the resources of connections and community. We also know that he is a father who is in deep pain because of his profound love for his gravely ill twelve-year-old daughter.

Look back to Mark 5:23 (Day 1, page 141). How does Jairus refer to his child?

For he had an only daughter, about twelve years old, who was dying.
(Luke 8:42a)

Now read Luke 8:42 in the margin. What do we learn about the child in Luke's account of the story?

The phrase "my little daughter" and the detail that she is Jairus's only child help us imagine the prayers Jairus might have prayed as he rushed to find Jesus, the healer:

"Please, God, my little girl. My baby. The tiny one I tickled and carried on my shoulders and tucked into bed. She's all we've got. Our only one. Please don't let her be taken from us."

While it may be common today for a family to have one child, in Jairus's culture it was the hope of each family to have many children—especially sons. Sons were a source of investment and stability, a way to make sure that you were taken care of in old age and that your business would be passed down. The more sons a family had, the better off they would be in the long run. A daughter would leave and join her husband's family upon marrying—something that was not too distant for a twelve-year-old daughter who would be coming of age very soon. So Jairus's reaction to his daughter's illness shows a love that goes beyond seeing her as an asset or possession—or even as a liability, as women were often seen in those days. His love for her is emotional and personal. She is precious to him.

Because Jairus is a man of respect and position, it would be considered improper for him to beg. So it is shocking for him to press through the common masses of people gathered around Jesus, shout to get Jesus' attention (as he surely has to do), fall at Jesus' feet, and beg repeatedly.

Apart from our two-for-one story, there is only one other instance in the Gospel of Mark where someone falls at Jesus' feet—a miracle story we studied last week.

Review the story of the Syrophoenician woman in Mark 7:24-30 (Week 4, page 126). What do you recall about how this woman was looked down on because of her nationality, religion, and gender?

Like the Syrophoenician woman, Jairus's love for his little daughter, who was precious to him, meant that he cared more for her than his own dignity and standing in society. He lowered himself to beg at the feet of a renegade rabbi, whose teaching and presence in Jairus's community was probably scandalous—including the very synagogue where Jairus was a leader. Love for a child can make someone cross all boundaries and give up everything if she or he believes it can help or save that child. Jairus is living proof. And Jesus responded with compassionate love, agreeing to go with Jairus even in the face of the worst news this desperate father could have received.

Now, just as Jesus did, let's turn our attention to the bleeding woman. While Jairus is named, we never learn her name. While Jairus is privileged, having status and connections in the community, she is alone and full of shame. Even her approach to Jesus seems to make her merely a disruption in a more important man's story—an inconvenient interruption when the life of a precious daughter is on the line.

This woman's story is one some people are uncomfortable with because of the nature of her disease: her bleeding for twelve years. If some can be uncomfortable naming it even today, then we have only a small view of what those in her own culture experienced. Her illness was no ordinary malady that would have allowed her family or community to surround her with care and help. In fact, there were laws devoted to women who were bleeding—not only as part of a regular menstrual cycle (see Leviticus 15:19) but also as an ongoing condition.

Read Leviticus 15:25-27, 31. What were the laws surrounding this woman's specific condition?

Extra Insight

The description of the bleeding woman's illness has made some wonder if she had a fistula, a condition that causes debilitating bleeding after complications in pregnancy or childbirth. This condition still plagues many women in developing countries today.

Because of the nature of her illness, this woman was not only sick; she was completely isolated. She lived alone and could not touch anyone. If she had a husband and perhaps even a child (see Extra Insight), she would not have been able to live with or touch them in twelve years.

Read Mark 5:26 (Day 1, page 141). What was the result of all her efforts to get help?

This desperate woman had tried everything to cure her illness, including spending *all* of her money and resources on doctors. But the attempted cures of primitive medicine might have been worse than the condition itself, because we're told that she only grew worse.

She knew better than to be in a crowd like this. The Jews considered her uncleanness contagious, and if anyone was to touch her, they would be spiritually and physically unclean too. If anyone in that crowd recognized her as stepping out of her rightful place, she would be revealed as putting the multitudes in danger and ostracized—perhaps even beaten or stoned.

Why would she take a risk like this? To put it very simply, she was desperate. She had *nothing* left to lose. She was beyond all hope and had exhausted every resource available to her. She must have heard about Jesus the healer, and she knew He was her last chance.

Has desperation ever led you to take a leap of faith at great risk? If so, describe it below:

While Jesus was literally on His way to help Jairus, she struggled through the crowd, got just close enough to this holy man, and reached out with her unclean hand to touch the most remote part of Him possible—the outermost piece of His clothing. Suddenly her body must have felt amazingly different and restored; the exhaustion, pain, and illness she had suffered for so long had flooded out of her and had been replaced by a new, powerful sense of wholeness and well-being. Jesus' cleanness had been more contagious than her uncleanness, and a mere touch brought restoration to her body. But at the same time, she was terrified because Jesus was looking around Him. "Who touched me?" He asked as He scanned the faces closest to Him.

She had shoplifted her healing—stolen power from the great I AM—and now He wanted to know who had done it.

Read Mark 5:33. How did she feel? What was her posture? And what did she tell Jesus?

What a terrifying feeling to know that someone so powerful could turn that power on you in a destructive way if that person chose to!

Unlike Jairus, who was someone of high status as a leader in the synagogue, this woman was a nobody. Being both a woman and someone with a spiritually unclean disease meant that she was not supposed to approach someone like Jesus for help. Yet both she and Jairus have come to the end of themselves and have nowhere else to turn. Desperation is the great equalizer. It puts all of us at the feet of Jesus, asking for His help.

Jairus's answered prayer will happen in a private home away from questioning eyes. Her healing happened in a very public place where she never wanted to be noticed. I wonder if the "whole truth" she told Jesus included the story of her illness, shame, isolation, and exhaustion. I wonder how much of it Jesus knew by just looking in her eyes. But instead of responding in anger, He looked down at her with compassion and spoke the word that changed her life forever.

Read Mark 5:34. How did Jesus address the woman?

What did He say had healed her, and what blessing did He speak over her?

Jesus called her *daughter*. How long had it been since anyone called her that—or spoken any word with kindness? This man, whose touch and words everyone was clamoring for, took time to look into her eyes. He took time to hear her "whole truth." He stopped the entire entourage—the surging crowd and the disciples whispering that He needed to hurry up because they were urgently on their way somewhere important to heal the daughter of a VIP who was dying. *She* was important enough for Him to stop everything.

> **Desperation is the great equalizer. It puts all of us at the feet of Jesus, asking for His help.**

Daughter. We've already heard that word spoken by a man who deeply loved his child. And Jairus's way of loving has shown us just what that word can mean: that a father could love a daughter enough that she was treasured beyond any value or collateral the world assigned to her; that a father could deem a daughter so valuable that he would leave his high position and lower himself if it meant she might be saved; that he would give anything if it meant sparing her life. The way Jairus felt about his little princess, his only daughter in the world who was so young that life for her had not really yet begun, is the way Jesus felt about this woman, who had been cast off by the world as if she had no value and dismissed as if her life was near the end.

Daughter. With that one word, Jesus tells her she is worth everything to Him. For twelve years Jairus's daughter had been treasured, loved, and spoiled. For twelve years this woman had been outcast, scorned, and rejected. One was cradled while the other was untouched. "Now," Jesus says, "you will know that you are treasured too. You are more than just healed; you are my daughter. Go in peace."

We long to hear these words, too. We long for relationship with our loving God, and the good news is that He longs for it too. Yet with all of the challenges, trials, and hurts we experience in life, we can struggle at times to feel completely loved and treasured.

Recall a time in your life when you've felt treasured, loved, and appreciated for exactly who you are. Who gave you that impression, and how?

Can you imagine God calling you *daughter* in the same way that Jesus gave the title to this woman? If not, what hinders you from believing God feels that way about you? If so, what helps you to understand God feels that way about you?

If you've ever felt unnoticed in a crowd, thought that someone else's requests were higher on God's priority list than yours, or had unanswered prayers that left you wondering if God even takes time to listen, then take a moment now to listen for Jesus' voice of compassion and love speaking tenderly and directly to you. Imagine the adoring look in His eyes as He looks into yours and whispers one word that changes everything: *Daughter!*

Talk with God

Oh, God, I am so in awe that You call me Your daughter. I belong to You! You know me and love me just as I am. And You have healing power just for me. You are so good. Speak to my heart when I feel like I am alone in my desperation. Remind me that I am Yours. In Jesus' name. Amen.

DAY 3: DEATH, WHERE IS YOUR STING?

Read God's Word

[38]*When they came to the house of the leader of the synagogue, [Jesus] saw a commotion, people weeping and wailing loudly.* [39]*When he had entered, he said to them, "Why do you make a commotion and weep? The child is not dead but sleeping."* [40]*And they laughed at him. Then he put them all outside, and took the child's father and mother and those who were with him, and went in where the child was.* [41]*He took her by the hand and said to her, "Talitha cum," which means, "Little girl, get up!"* [42]*And immediately the girl got up and began to walk about (she was twelve years of age). At this they were overcome with amazement.*

(Mark 5:38-42)

Reflect and Respond

In our two-for-one miracle story we've seen not only the threat of death but the reality of death. I'll never forget the very first funeral that I presided over as a pastor. I stood in the pulpit, looking out over a sea of grieving, tear-streaked faces, and read this passage from First Corinthians:

> *"Death has been swallowed up in victory."*
> *"Where, O death, is your victory?*
> *Where, O death, is your sting?"*
> *(1 Corinthians 15:54-55)*

I remember thinking, What a ridiculous question! These people know exactly where the sting of death is. They are hurting from it right now. The person they love is gone and they would do anything to bring her back.

Besides presiding as a pastor before other families who have felt cheated by death, I myself have stood where they stand. I've felt the deep pain and loss for family members gone too soon, most memorably my younger cousin Brian, who died tragically at twenty-one years old the day before Christmas Eve. As any

family who's had a time of shock and deep loss can attest, that anniversary and the memory of Brian's loss will always be a part of our Christmas memories. The sting of death, even with healing over the years, is still remembered especially on that day each year.

The sting of death has driven all of us to desperate places. Loss and grief are some of the most common elements of the human experience, and yet when we go through them, it seems as if no one else can understand the depth of our pain.

But Jesus understands the depth of our pain. He experienced the loss of those closest to Him: His cousin John the Baptist was brutally killed by a tyrant, and we know His own earthly father, Joseph, probably died somewhere in his youth or young adulthood, since he is not present in any Gospel stories past Jesus' twelfth year. When we witness Jesus' own witnessing of death and loss, we see a heart filled with human compassion. We also see a God who loves His children so much that He will do anything to take down the adversary of death.

While we watch Jesus in isolated battles with death throughout His ministry, there is a greater war being waged. God began the world as a place where death had no place in the unspoiled creation that was His perfect will. So in order to return His people to a place with no more death or mourning or crying or pain (Revelation 21:4), Jesus undertook a comprehensive campaign of war against death itself!

Actually, death is not just a single event experienced once in each of our lives. Dr. Joseph Dongell imagines death as an octopus,[2] operating multiple tentacles to draw prey toward destruction. According to this picture, while we may not always recognize these different facets as being tentacles or extensions of death's scheme, they are unified and cooperative, under the control of a single power. He suggests that the major tentacles of death are:

- Satan and his demons
- human structures of injustice, evil, violence, and warfare
- sin itself, with its own corrupting and corrosive effects
- sickness and disease of all kinds (including mental illnesses and addictions)
- human ignorance, both in general and in relation to God's truth and love
- nature turned destructive (e.g., storms, earthquakes, volcanoes, drought, fire, flood)[3]

Death is the ultimate goal or outcome of each of these tentacles or schemes—though it is easier to recognize in some of them than in others. All lead toward the destruction of people, relationships, and communities and therefore are the tools of death itself.

In the Scriptures we see Jesus doing everything in His power to combat each of these extensions of death and ultimately reach His final goal: to destroy death itself. He demonstrates power to overcome all of these tentacles through:

Casting out evil spirits

Justice

Forgiveness

Healing

Teaching

Rescue

Stop for a moment and make a note beside any of these things you've witnessed Jesus doing, either in Scripture (perhaps some of the miracles we've studied so far) or in your own experience.

All of these powerful acts are ways that Jesus battles the enemy of death. Of course, the ultimate power Jesus exhibits over death is resurrection, the fundamental *reversal* of death itself. Jesus' own resurrection from the tomb is the culmination of His ministry on earth. It shows us that He has broken the power of death itself and now makes a way for us to live eternally with Him.

But along the way in His ministry, Jesus also breaks the power of death by raising back to life three people: Jairus's daughter, the son of the widow of Nain, and his dear friend Lázarus. Some people describe these as resurrections, while others use the word *resuscitation* or *re-animation*, wanting to distinguish resurrection as something that happens to us only once when we are restored to life in Christ eternally. It's true that all three persons Jesus brought back to life eventually died again; but if they had faith in Christ, they found themselves experiencing resurrection and eternal life. So for our study, we'll simply refer to these three persons as those that Jesus raised from the dead.

The first one we are familiar with already: Jairus's daughter. She was a mere twelve years old when a fatal illness took her life. Her father went to great trouble to get Jesus' attention and beg Jesus to come back to His home, but on their way Jesus was distracted by the case of the bleeding woman. I imagine that when Jairus received word that they were too late, that his daughter was already dead, he felt a deep sense of loss and grief. He also may have felt disappointment in Jesus or in himself for failing to get there soon enough.

> The ultimate power Jesus exhibits over death is resurrection, the fundamental *reversal* of death itself.

Extra Insight

In the culture at that time, this widow would have been left completely destitute without the support of a husband or son. In addition to her personal grief, her own life would be in danger since she may not have had family or financial provision.

¹²As he approached the gate of the town, a man who had died was being carried out. He was his mother's only son, and she was a widow; and with her was a large crowd from the town. ¹³When the Lord saw her, he had compassion for her and said to her, "Do not weep."

(Luke 7:12-13)

---

⁸ The disciples said to him, "Rabbi, the Jews were just now trying to stone you, and are you going there again?" … ¹⁶ Thomas, who was called the Twin, said to his fellow disciples, "Let us also go, that we may die with him."

(John 11:8, 16)

Think of a time when someone close to you died. Describe the emotions you felt at first, including how you felt toward God (not what you *believed*, but how you *felt*):

The moment Jesus took the hand of Jairus's little girl and helped her rise from her deathbed must have been the most astonishing and joyful moment of her parents' lives!

Another incidence of Jesus restoring someone to their family occurs in the seventh chapter of Luke. While in other stories family members request Jesus' help, this time Jesus happens upon a funeral and initiates the restorative encounter Himself. This time it is a widow who is fresh in grief over her only son.

Read Luke 7:12-13 in the margin. What touches Jesus, moving Him to have compassion? What does He say to her?

The central figure of this story seems to be the mother herself, and once Jesus commands the young man to rise, he sits up and begins to talk. Then we read, "Jesus gave him to his mother" (Luke 7:15). Jesus is healing not only the disordered body of the dead person but also restoring broken hearts and families.

Finally, Jesus faces the death of a personal friend, Lazarus. Jesus knows his friend's family well and has visited them before; but when He is asked to return to Bethany where Lazarus is gravely ill, the disciples discourage Jesus from going.

Read John 11: 8 and 16 in the margin. Why do the disciples not want Jesus to go to Jerusalem?

By the time Jesus arrives, Lazarus is dead and has been in the tomb for four days. Jesus faces the anger of Lazarus's sister Martha for delaying His arrival (John 11:21-27), as well as His own grief over the loss of His dear friend.

Read John 11:33-35 in the margin. Why was Jesus deeply moved? What did He do in response?

Now read John 11:43-44 in the margin. How did Jesus raise Lazarus from the dead?

33When Jesus saw [Mary] weeping, and the Jews who came with her also weeping, he was greatly disturbed in spirit and deeply moved. 34He said, "Where have you laid him?" They said to him, "Lord, come and see." 35Jesus began to weep.

(John 11:33-35)

43[Jesus] cried with a loud voice, "Lazarus, come out!" 44The dead man came out, his hands and feet bound with strips of cloth, and his face wrapped in a cloth. Jesus said to them, "Unbind him, and let him go."

(John 11:43-44)

What can we notice when looking at all three of these stories together? I'd like to highlight four insights that reveal the compassionate heart of our Lord and the power of His love.

1. *The magnitude of their loss gives us understanding of God's own sacrifice.* Jairus and the widow both experience the death of their *only* child, and Mary and Martha are grieving for their *only* brother. The scarcity expressed here amplifies our understanding of just how devastated they are, and the repeated mention of the death of an only child helps us understand God's ultimate sacrifice that will come soon after these stories when "he gave his only Son" (John 3:16).

2. *Jesus experienced grief just as we do.* Overflowing grief and tears abound in each of these stories. Ultimately, Jesus Himself weeps for His friend (John 11:35)—and possibly for the fact that He knows His own personal experience with death is on its way. Scripture affirms our deep emotions of love and grief by showing us Jesus experiencing the same emotions.

3. *We see Jesus' power over death.* In each story, Jesus commands the person to rise with His words. This may be an echo back to the Creation story, where God creates and produces life by speaking things into existence. It also shows Jesus' definitive power and command over death.

4. *God's timing is often not our timing.* We see that relatives in these stories are sometimes frustrated with the timing of Jesus' miracles. We will also find ourselves wishing God had met our expectations and not understanding His plans, but just as they can trust Him, we can too. Why? Because He loves us so deeply.

As we saw in Lazarus's story, Jesus is "deeply moved in spirit and troubled" by the grief of those He loves (John 11:33 NIV). This is one of my favorite details from Lazarus's story. The Greek word for the state Jesus was in is *embrimaomai*, which can literally mean the snorting of a horse![4] This could have been heard as a shudder or a groan, but the imagery is one of a powerful horse raging to go into battle. Jesus is actually "chomping at the bit" to take on death once and for all!

Jesus experienced grief just as we do.

Jesus opposes the tentacles of death at every turn. With every miracle, He strikes another blow against His opponent. But He knows that the only thing that will bring the decisive upset will be His own death—and then the defeat of death through His resurrection. While He could have gone on raising person after person from the grave, the truth is that each person would eventually die again. He knew that if He actually entered death Himself and won, He would defeat the enemy that faces each of us and be able to bring us into eternity with Him, where death no longer has power over us.

I know what it's like to mourn the loss of someone I love. You do too. Death is a part of all our lives, and it's sometimes hard to remember the deep truths of God when the sting of death is so personal and so fresh. But the words of 1 Corinthians 15 can help remind us of Jesus' victory until we all can say them together in eternity. Whether I'm presiding over a funeral or reading the words to myself in my own time of need, I say them with confidence yet also with compassion, acknowledging that we can say what is true even if we don't yet *feel* it at the time. We can say it because He fought death for us, and won!

> 54"*Death has been swallowed up in victory.*"
> 55"*Where, O death, is your victory?*
> *Where, O death, is your sting?*"

> 56*The sting of death is sin, and the power of sin is the law.* 57*But thanks be to God, who gives us the victory through our Lord Jesus Christ.*

(1 Corinthians 15:54b-57)

Talk with God

Loving God, I know that You fought death for us and won, but I also know the grief we all feel when we say goodbye to those we have loved. The truth is that death can feel really final here. Seal these Scriptures in my heart so I remember that You weep over those You love, understand our tears and sadness, and fought for us so that we have an eternal hope. In Jesus' name. Amen.

DAY 4: MOVED WITH COMPASSION

Read God's Word

30*Immediately aware that power had gone forth from him, Jesus turned about in the crowd and said, "Who touched my clothes?"* 31*And his disciples said to him, "You see the crowd pressing in on you; how can you say, 'Who touched me?'"* 32*He looked all around to see who had done it.* 33*But the woman, knowing what had happened to her, came in fear and trembling, fell down before him, and told him the whole truth.* 34*He* *said to her, "Daughter, your faith has made you well; go in peace, and be healed of your disease."*

(Mark 5:30-34)

[40]*A man with leprosy came and knelt in front of Jesus, begging to be healed. "If you are willing, you can heal me and make me clean," he said.*

[41]*Moved with compassion, Jesus reached out and touched him. "I am willing," he said. "Be healed!" *[42]*Instantly the leprosy disappeared, and the man was healed.*

(Mark 1:40-42 NLT)

Reflect and Respond

When I visit churches around the country, I'm fascinated by how different they are from one another. Somehow, for the singular purpose of worshiping God, we have created incredibly different spaces: warehouses with metal chairs and gritty floors, cathedrals with stained glass and dark wood, chapels with white steeples and worn pews.

I'm especially captivated by different works of art I find there depicting Jesus. Seeing Jesus' face reflected in paintings or stained glass or even modern art installations makes me study His expression a little closer and wonder, *What side of Jesus did the artist want us to see? How is Jesus feeling in this moment? If this portrait could speak, what would Jesus say?* Every single portrait is different, and every one is an artist's representation of what he or she believed about Jesus. Was He serious? Angry or upset? Sometimes He is smiling or looking amused. A handful of times I have seen Jesus depicted as laughing. Yet although we know it happened, I can't even think of one occasion when I've seen a painting of Jesus crying.

Jesus was filled with emotion. His interactions with people show deeply held feelings and wonderfully personal reactions. Consider the two-for-one story we've immersed ourselves in this week—of Jesus healing the bleeding woman and raising Jairus's daughter from the dead. When I picture Jesus in this story, I can't imagine a wooden, unfeeling Jesus speaking His lines as if they were written on cue cards. When Jesus sees Jairus's reaction at the news that his daughter has died or locks eyes with the woman in the crowd, He *feels* for them. His heart is tender, and He is filled with compassion. He connects with their emotions, feels empathy, and offers His best to reach their worst.

God heals because He loves. He created our world in love, and now He lovingly works to restore the brokenness of His creation. When He heals, Jesus engages in great acts of power. But healing is not ultimately about power. Healing is about love.[5]

God heals because He loves. . . . Healing is not ultimately about power. Healing is about love.

The Greek word often used to describe Jesus' compassion is pronounced *splancÚizomai*. (If you say it out loud, someone may respond with "God bless you!") It means "to be affected deeply in one's inner being (bowels)."[6]

This word is so unusual that although it's often translated "moved with compassion" (such as in Mark 1:41 NLT above), it also is translated "Jesus was indignant" (NIV). This compassion is so deep that it provokes a visceral, physical response (thus the referral to feeling it deep in one's bowels).

This kind of compassion will not be still. It evokes a response. Every time someone in the Gospels is described as having this kind of compassion, he or she is moved. Literally, he or she moves toward the one he or she feels compassion for, and that person responds.

In the Gospels, Jesus feels and acts on compassion by moving toward the people in deep need that He encounters. Before many of the miracles, He displays or is described as having this compassion that leads to action. The deep emotion that Jesus feels when He encounters desperation leads Him to act in power.

Let's look at three miracles preceded by Jesus' *splanchnizomai* compassion. Though we've looked at each of these miracles previously in our study, here we are focusing our gaze on the compassion that motivates His response.

1. *Jesus heals a leper* (Mark 1:41-42 and Luke 5:12-16). Jesus' compassion is so great that He risks reaching out a hand to touch a leper. In Mark's account, we're told explicitly of Jesus' compassion: "*Moved with compassion*, Jesus reached out and touched him" (Mark 1:41 NLT, emphasis added). His compassion is so visceral, in fact, that some translations describe it as indignation or anger: "Jesus was *indignant*. He reached out his hand and touched the man. 'I am willing,' he said. 'Be clean!'" (Mark 1:41 NIV, emphasis added). Sometimes our compassion is expressed as a holy indignation that means we are compelled to help remedy something that is wrong.

2. *Jesus heals a grieving widow* (Luke 7:11-15). Here Jesus' heart is touched by the grieving widow of Nain who has lost her only son. "When the Lord saw her, *his heart went out to her* and he said, 'Don't cry'" (Luke 7:13 NIV, emphasis added). While the physical healing in this story is to restore the body of a dead son, the focus of compassion and the healing gift are for the mother.

3. *Jesus heals a demon-possessed boy* (Mark 9:14-27). Here the father of the boy begs Jesus to look on them with this kind of compassion: "Jesus asked the boy's father, 'How long has he been like this?' 'From childhood,' he answered. 'It has often thrown him into fire or water to kill him. But if you can do anything, *take pity on us* and help us'" (Mark 9:21-22 NIV, emphasis added). Jesus' questions about the boy's condition let the father know He had a deep interest and wanted to help.

> The deep emotion that Jesus feels when He encounters desperation leads Him to act in power.

Can you think of other examples in the New Testament of this kind of compassion that moves someone to action? If so, note them below:

Jesus is the only living person in the Gospels described as being "moved with compassion" (*splanchnizomai*) in this way. But He also told stories that attributed this kind of compassion to fictional characters. In three different stories that Jesus told, He described a main figure as being "moved" with this kind of compassion.[7]

As you read a portion of each parable, (1) circle the name or role of the person who has compassion, (2) underline the words that were translated from the Greek word *splanchnizomai,* indicating that someone was "filled with compassion" or "took pity," and (3) put parentheses around the action that person was "moved" to do.

The parable of the unmerciful servant:

"The servant's master took pity on him, canceled the debt and let him go."

(Matthew 18:27 NIV)

The parable of the good Samaritan:

[33]"A Samaritan, as he traveled, came where the man was; and when he saw him, he took pity on him. [34]He went to him and bandaged his wounds, pouring on oil and wine. Then he put the man on his own donkey, brought him to an inn and took care of him."

(Luke 10:33-34 NIV)

The parable of the prodigal son:

"While he was still a long way off, his father saw him and was filled with compassion for him; he ran to his son, threw his arms around him and kissed him."

(Luke 15:20 NIV)

Compassion leads to action. In each of these stories, Jesus was spinning an illustration of what it means to feel deep compassion and then act on it by treating someone else with kindness and care. Jesus could tell these stories with authority and authenticity because He Himself experienced compassion and acted on it.

Compassion leads to action.

In these stories, Jesus is explaining what compassion looks like: a master forgiving outstanding debts, a traveler healing the wounds of a stranger who cannot pay him back, and a father running to his son despite the wrongs that son has done. Jesus not only told these stories to explain compassion; He then starred in them. He enacted the role of pardoner of debt, healer of wounds, and joyfully forgiving father.

Jesus' teachings and miracles are not two separate entities that happened to occur on the same road trips. They are two ways of communicating the same truth about God made visible in His Son—and that is His incredible compassion.

Jesus also displayed compassion in the crowds that He taught.

Read Matthew 9:35-36 in the margin. Why did Jesus have compassion on the crowds that He encountered as He was teaching and healing?

35Jesus went through all the towns and villages, teaching in their synagogues, proclaiming the good news of the kingdom and healing every disease and sickness. 36When he saw the crowds, he had compassion on them, because they were harassed and helpless, like sheep without a shepherd.

(Matthew 9:35-36 NIV)

In another crowd scene, at the feeding of five thousand, Jesus again felt and acted on deep compassion for the crowd.

Read Mark 6:34 in the margin. Why did Jesus have compassion in this instance?

When Jesus landed and saw a large crowd, he had compassion on them, because they were like sheep without a shepherd. So he began teaching them many things.

(Mark 6:34 NIV)

As a result of His compassion, Jesus began teaching the people and eventually fed them as well.

Shepherds are responsible for the care, feeding, and protection of their sheep. They are herders, taking care of huge numbers of animals at once. But Jesus also told of a shepherd who prized the needs of one sheep who strayed away from the herd: "Suppose one of you has a hundred sheep and loses one of them. Doesn't he leave the ninety-nine in the open country and go after the lost sheep until he finds it?" (Luke 15:4 NIV).

This is the kind of shepherding we see enacted by Jesus again and again. He cares for the crowds, but also sees the needs of an individual that He can help, and He zeroes in on the person's desperation as He works toward a solution. We see exactly this side of Jesus in the Mark 5 story of Jairus's daughter and the outcast woman Jesus honors with the name *daughter*. As we've seen previously, when Jairus falls at Jesus' feet in desperation, looking for help for his dying daughter, Jesus immediately leaves the crowd and goes with him. And when the woman touches Jesus' cloak and He feels power leave Him, He stops everything to find her in the crowd and takes time to hear her story. Instead of just curing her, Jesus heals her. He speaks life to her, including declaring publicly that she is well—a priestly statement that would restore her to her family and community.

Compassion cares for the crowds, but when there is an individual who has a deep and desperate need, compassion is not afraid to turn and focus energy and resources and love until that need is heard and cared for.

You are more than a number in a crowd to Jesus. When He sees your anguish and pain, He has this kind of moving compassion for you. It's more than a feeling; it results in action—the action of God's grace and mercy expressed in your life.

Have people or situations ever stirred this kind of deep compassion within you? If so, what do you do when you feel this compassion?

When you feel compassion toward others, you can recall these stories and mirror the look you imagine in Jesus' eyes in these instances. You can see the individuals instead of letting them get lost in the crowd. You can ask questions about their feelings and needs. And you can pray for them.

Sometimes when we pray for people, they are not physically healed. But through prayer they always receive Jesus' compassion. Prayer is one of the best ways to show love and compassion for someone. It is carrying the ones we love to the One whose compassion moves heaven and earth.

Talk with God

Lord, I have prayed for friends and loved ones who were not physically healed. I don't understand why, but I believe that You are full of compassion—that my prayers and the prayers of others were heard and answered. I believe that we aren't lost in a crowd of hurting people—that You see us and know exactly what we need. Thank You for taking good care of me. I am desperate for You. Amen.

DAY 5: THE ALREADY-NOT-YET KINGDOM

Read God's Word

[18]*John's disciples told him about all these things. Calling two of them,* [19]*he sent them to the Lord to ask, "Are you the one who is to come, or should we expect someone else?"*

> You are more than a number in a crowd to Jesus. When He sees your anguish and pain, He has . . . compassion for you.

> The healings of Christ were also confirmation of His compassionate plan for all of God's people— God's plan to redeem the world through Christ.

[20]When the men came to Jesus, they said, "John the Baptist sent us to you to ask, 'Are you the one who is to come, or should we expect someone else?'"

[21]At that very time Jesus cured many who had diseases, sicknesses and evil spirits, and gave sight to many who were blind. [22]So he replied to the messengers, "Go back and report to John what you have seen and heard: The blind receive sight, the lame walk, those who have leprosy are cleansed, the deaf hear, the dead are raised, and the good news is proclaimed to the poor. [23]Blessed is anyone who does not stumble on account of me."

(Luke 7:18-23 NIV)

Reflect and Respond

For two weeks now we have looked extensively at the healing miracles of Jesus. Last week we took notice of the restoration and wholeness that He brought to the lives of those He healed, and this week we've marveled at the compassionate love that led to the actions of healing we've witnessed in His ministry. Countless lives were touched by Jesus' healing miracles, but healing was always more than an individual gift. Today as we wrap up our study on this theme, we will see that the healings of Christ were also confirmation of His compassionate plan for all of God's people—God's plan to redeem the world through Christ.

We know from Matthew's Gospel account that Jesus' cousin John the Baptist was in prison (Matthew 11:2), and word was getting back to John about Jesus' miraculous actions. Picking up the story in the Gospel of Luke, we learn that John sent a couple of his own disciples to ask Jesus: "Are you the one who is to come, or should we expect someone else?" (Luke 7:20 NIV). What did he mean by "are you the one who is to come"?

John's entire ministry has been preparing the way for the Messiah, the One who would come to rescue God's people. John had spent his life telling people about the Messiah. There had been some wonderful clues that these hopes were being fulfilled in his younger cousin, Jesus. He had witnessed the Spirit of the Lord descend on Jesus when he baptized Him. He had pointed the way to Jesus and declared: "Look, the Lamb of God, who takes away the sin of the world!" (John 1:29 NIV). And yet, he still had to ask: "Are you the one? Are you the Messiah?"

I can imagine John, unjustly imprisoned and knowing that he would probably die there behind the prison walls yet reaching out to Jesus. John had offended a king who was known for his erratic and cruel actions, and the outlook for his survival was not good. He wanted to know at the end of his life and ministry if he had been right about Jesus. He also was hearing remarkable stories about Jesus' miraculous actions and needed to know firsthand if they were true—if they were signs that the Messiah had finally come to rescue God's people.

When John asks, "Are you the one?" Jesus sends back a message. He tells John's disciples to report what they have witnessed, what they have personally seen and heard.

Look back at Luke 22. What are the miracles Jesus lists as evidence?

1.

2.

3.

4.

5.

6.

These signs of the Messiah's coming have been anticipated from the time of the prophets.

Read Isaiah 35:5-6 in the margin. What kinds of miracles are promised when the Messiah comes to save God's people?

How many of these miracles have we witnessed Jesus performing in our study?

Then the eyes of the blind shall be opened,
and the ears of the deaf unstopped;
⁶ then the lame shall leap like a deer,
and the tongue of the speechless sing for joy.
For waters shall break forth in the wilderness,
and streams in the desert.
(Isaiah 35:5-6)

So, God's people could take the sign of miraculous healings as more than individual instances of Jesus' care and compassion. Jesus, indeed, had care and compassion for individuals, but these healings also were a sign that the kingdom of God was breaking into the kingdom of this world and defeating the signs of evil, sin, and death.

John the Baptist himself had preached a message about the nearness of the kingdom of God. He traveled around the wilderness of Judea proclaiming, "Repent, for the kingdom of heaven has come near" (Matthew 3:2).

While we recognize signs—including the miracles of Jesus—as indications that the kingdom of God is present in our midst, another reality is that God's kingdom is not yet fully here. We call this the paradox of "already/not yet."

Understanding that Jesus is already Lord of this world but that the world does not yet look or function as God wants it to helps us understand things like healing. We know not everyone will be healed in our "not yet" world. We know that not everything will look or function the way God wants it to. We know that we will find ourselves desperate for Jesus to work a miracle. But we are looking forward to a day when we can proclaim the triumphant words of Revelation 11:15, which are included in George Frideric Handel's "Hallelujah Chorus": "The kingdom of this world is become the kingdom of our Lord, and of His Christ." What kinds of healing miracles can we expect from our Lord, our healer and rescuer, in this already/not yet world? In his book *Experiencing Healing and Wholeness*, Dr. Donald Demaray outlines five miracles of healing that he witnessed in his ministry of healing as a pastor and professor.[8] Let's consider each one so that we recognize and call out the healing work of God when we see it in its many forms.

1. *The miracle of supernatural touch*

This kind of miracle is usually what comes to our minds when we talk about healing or ask God for healing. Sometimes it's instantaneous and other times gradual. When we witness healing that is not explainable by modern medicine, we shouldn't try to rationalize or explain it away. God is still at work healing people today.

Some years ago, I found myself in friendships with a handful of women close to my own age who were physicians, although they didn't know one another. Maybe it was my own love for medicine and science that drew me into each of these friendships or the commonalities and struggles we shared as professional moms, but I really enjoyed each of these women and wanted them to know and enjoy one another, so I arranged a dinner where they could all meet. To my delight, they did enjoy one another's company, and the things they had in common to talk about were fascinating. In those friendships I would sometimes hear in hushed tones stories from their medical practice that had no logical scientific explanation. While medicine would expect one result, the patient's response would be inexplicably (and miraculously) better. As a pastor who works in the world of prayers and "it's all in God's hands," it was exciting to hear stories from doctors who were expected to provide medical results but who had witnessed God's hands in action.

Is it difficult or easy for you to believe in miracles that do not have a scientific or rational explanation? Why?

Have you ever witnessed a supernatural miracle? If so, describe what happened below:

2. The miracle of the doctor and modern medicine

The wisdom and virtuousness that inspire people to use their gifts to develop treatments, medicines, and cures for diseases are God-given gifts. Throughout history Christians have been so concerned for health and wholeness that many of the hospitals and clinics around the world have been founded in Christ's name.

As a pastor, I have lost track of the number of people I have visited in hospitals and surgical suites before their surgeries or medical procedures. Often as I have been about to pray with them, doctors and nurses and other medical personnel would come in and out of the room, going about their business. I would sometimes invite those professionals to join us in prayer, and often sensed a deep gratitude when they heard me praying for their hands to be instruments of God's healing work. Many medical professionals recognize that the gifts they wield are from the Lord, who is our ultimate healer.

Describe a time when you have experienced or witnessed the miracle of modern medicine:

How did you experience God's peace in this situation?

3. The miracle of the healing powers of the human body

It's an amazing thing to witness how often the body heals itself. Even much of modern medicine prescribes rest and patience so that the body can repair damage and disease. This is a work of God! When my children have cuts and scrapes that we notice are getting better day by day (usually at bath time), I often tell them, "Look at that: God is healing you." My five-year-old daughter noticed an old scratch on her body the other day, and before I could say a word she repeated the words back to me that I've often told her: "Look, Mommy! Jesus is healing me!" We need to recognize and praise God for the ways our human bodies do work within His plans, even as we pray for areas that are broken or sick.

> We need to recognize and praise God for the ways our human bodies do work within His plans, even as we pray for areas that are broken or sick.

Recall a recent example of this kind of natural healing that you have either experienced or witnessed. Think about the miraculous ability of the human body to repair itself, and write a prayer of praise and thanksgiving to God below:

4. The miracle of "my grace is sufficient for you"

Sometimes people are not physically healed. Their illness or suffering can go on for extended periods of time no matter how many people pray. But God can bring victory in suffering. In their desperation, people who are suffering often come to rely on God more than ever, and they are changed in ways that those of us who do not know suffering are not. Those who bear struggles with sick or broken bodies are often given gifts of peace, patience, love, and faith while they pray and lean on God.

One woman I knew suffered for years with a painful and degenerative disease. She told me that in the early days she would pray to God: "Lord, if you will take away this disease, I will love you and serve you always." She tried to bargain with God and felt that the only way to move forward with life was if the disease was miraculously removed from her. Finally, she told me, she began to pray: "Lord, even if you never take away this disease, I will love you and serve you always." The state of her body had not changed, but the state of her soul had. She had received the gift of seeing that she had been given all that was sufficient to live in God's grace.

Look up Psalm 41:3 and 2 Corinthians 12:7-10. What do these verses say about God's sufficient grace in our struggles?

When have you experienced or witnessed the miracle of God's grace? How was God's peace present to you?

5. *The miracle of the victorious crossing*

Scripture tells us that in death there is no more pain or suffering. In fact, in eternity even death is no more. This is the ultimate healing. Dr. Donald Demaray, who wrote and taught about these categories of healing, was my professor. I even took his class on the theology of healing. He died last year, joining his beloved wife who preceded him in death. I think of him often, and how he encouraged us to find joy in the anticipation of eternity with Jesus. I picture him sitting with Jesus, smiling and having afternoon tea—which he did every day—and humming the "Hallelujah Chorus," the song that for him showed the greatest triumph in God's kingdom.

How does thinking of this ultimate miracle of healing give you comfort, hope, and peace?

Healing comes in many forms, but it is always a confirmation of God's care and compassion for us. His presence is with us no matter our circumstances. Healing is also a sign that God's kingdom is both here and on its way in fullness. God's love for you is greater than any circumstance or struggle you are going through. Never forget that His love is a rescuing, healing love, and that He has declared His overwhelming love for *you*!

Talk with God

Your love is amazing, God. Your compassion is endless, and Your mercies are new every morning. When I can't see You moving, when I can't hear Your voice, when I am wondering where You are—draw me closer to You. Help me to lean in to Your compassion. Thank You so much that Your love for me is greater than any circumstance or struggle I might face. In Jesus' name. Amen.

God's love for you is greater than any circumstance or struggle you are going through.

Mark 5:25-29

Desperation is a __gift__ sometimes.

Mark 5:30-34

Jesus wants a __Relationship__ with us.

We can feel __Left__ __out__ when we hear how God has healed or blessed others.

Jesus shows us that nothing, not even __death__, can stop Him.

Week 6

THE GRAND MIRACLE

Jesus Himself

DAY 1: YOU ARE MY MIRACLE

Read God's Word

²⁶In the sixth month the angel Gabriel was sent by God to a town in Galilee called Nazareth, ²⁷to a virgin engaged to a man whose name was Joseph, of the house of David. The virgin's name was Mary. ²⁸And he came to her and said, "Greetings, favored one! The Lord is with you." ²⁹But she was much perplexed by his words and pondered what sort of greeting this might be. ³⁰The angel said to her, "Do not be afraid, Mary, for you have found favor with God. ³¹And now, you will conceive in your womb and bear a son, and you will name him Jesus. ³²He will be great, and will be called the Son of the Most High, and the Lord God will give to him the throne of his ancestor David. ³³He will reign over the house of Jacob forever, and of his kingdom there will be no end." ³⁴Mary said to the angel, "How can this be, since I am a virgin?" ³⁵The angel said to her, "The Holy Spirit will come upon you, and the power of the Most High will overshadow you; therefore the child to be born will be holy; he will be called Son of God. ³⁶And now, your relative Elizabeth in her old age has also conceived a son; and this is the sixth month for her who was said to be barren. ³⁷For nothing will be impossible with God." ³⁸Then Mary said, "Here am I, the servant of the Lord; let it be with me according to your word." Then the angel departed from her.

(Luke 1:26-38)

Reflect and Respond

A pastor was thumbing through the prayer request cards people had dropped in the offering plates that Sunday and found one written by a ten-year-old:

Dear Jesus, thank you for keeping us in your loving heart. Thank you for giving all of these different miracles from learning to ride your bike to putting footsteps on the moon. We thank you for giving us food to eat and fresh water to drink. You do so much for us that we can't thank you back. You are my miracle. Amen.

(Alex, Age 10)

Alex must have had miracles on his mind that day. He wanted to thank God for the simplest act that seemed like a miracle to him—learning to ride a bike—to the most awe inspiring: walking on the moon. He recognized that there was way more to thank God for than he could begin to mention. But then he mentioned one thing that seemed to capture all the blessings into one. I can't get over the simple and profound way that he put it: "You are my miracle."

It's true, isn't it? Jesus Himself is a miracle. The very existence and identity of God who became human, who walked and laughed and ate and slept and stubbed His toe—all of that is itself a singular miracle.

This last week together we're going to look at the miracles of Jesus through the lens of the miracle that is Jesus Himself. The miracle of Jesus' identity as both fully God and fully human is called the *Incarnation*. It's one of the simplest truths of the Christian faith yet possibly one of the hardest to wrap our minds around.

In Jesus, God and humanity have become one. How can this even be possible? To define God is to paint categories that are outside of human possibility. He is without limits in His knowledge (omniscience), location (omnipresence), and power (omnipotence). As humans, we are all too aware of our own limits in those categories and many more.

While we often accept the truth of Jesus' identity without question, it can be one of the hardest truths to understand or explain. One of the brightest biblical scholars I know says so: "Incarnation is not something that human beings can fully get their mental calipers around. It involves miracle and mystery, and is frankly above our mental pay grade, even for the brightest amongst us."[1]

Yet my five-year-old daughter and my ninety-six-year-old grandmother both grasp the truth of Jesus' identity with ease. They both adore Jesus, talk about Him with a familiarity, and revere Him as holy. Both of them are my teachers as I seek to understand more about having a relationship with Jesus, because they both approach Him with a simplicity that is effortless. Ask my daughter if Jesus is God, and her answer is yes. Ask her if Jesus is a person, and you'll get the same answer: yes. Jesus makes sense to her even before she can spell His name.

When an angel appeared to Mary and announced her role in the Incarnation, she had trouble grasping just what was going to happen. Most of us would have too! But God comforted and assured her of His presence and His purposes.

Review today's passage, Luke 1:26-38. What are some of the promises of God's presence or power?

What are some of Mary's reactions?

Extra Insight

Omniscience – God is all-knowing

Omnipresence – God is everywhere

Omnipotence – God is all-powerful

What aspects of this passage are miraculous?

From the beginning, God's incarnation was tough to grapple with, but His promises were reassurances of His presence, His favor, and His success. The angel told Mary that "nothing will be impossible with God" (Luke 1:37); another translation says, "No word from God will ever fail" (NIV), and Jesus would be the very Word of God (John 1:1). This crazy sounding plan of the unification of God and man would be a success.

Read John 1:14 in the margin. What would the Word become? And where would He live?

The Word became flesh and lived among us, and we have seen his glory, the glory as of a father's only son, full of grace and truth.

(John 1:14)

Write the verse in your own words below:

The word for "lived among us" or "dwelt among us" was the Greek word *skenoo*, literally meaning "to pitch a tent."[2] This verse could be translated "The Word became flesh and pitched his tent in our camp alongside our tents." God was taking on the tent of flesh and neurons and skin cells and taste buds and muscle fibers and DNA. And with all the great things about the human condition, He also was pledging to take on influenza and chicken pox and grief and rejection and pain and, ultimately, death.

God's people had traveled in the wilderness with a tabernacle where God lived among them (Exodus 40:34-35), so this concept of God in a tent was nothing new. Only this time the tent God would inhabit was a human being, who would encounter every temptation and trial that can come to the human nature. God was taking on the struggles we have as human beings along with our DNA.

In early Christianity, as people were working out what the church believed and how to understand difficult truths, most of the major heresies—beliefs contrary to what the church came to accept as truth—centered around misunderstandings of who Jesus was. As people tried to explain Jesus' identity, they tipped too far to one side or the other—either believing that "Jesus was so fully God that He really wasn't human after all but was just occupying a human container" or that "Jesus was so human that He wasn't fully God but just a person that God made." Some people were unbalanced in their understanding of the Incarnation, but the church insisted that Jesus was 100 percent God and 100 percent human all at once.

Clarity on the identity and life of Jesus was one of the main reasons the church established the creeds. The Apostles' Creed states what we believe about God the Father in two lines ("I believe in God the Father Almighty, maker of heaven and earth") and what we believe about the Holy Spirit in one simple line: "I believe in the Holy Spirit."[3] It doesn't get much simpler than that! Yet what we believe about Jesus is retold in *ten* lines:

> I believe in Jesus Christ, his only Son, our Lord,
>   who was conceived by the Holy Spirit,
>   born of the Virgin Mary,
>   suffered under Pontius Pilate,
>   was crucified, died, and was buried;
>   he descended to the dead.
>   On the third day he rose again;
>   he ascended into heaven,
>   is seated at the right hand of the Father,
>   and he will come again to judge the living and the dead.[4]

So much space is given to Jesus in the creed not because one member of the Trinity is more important than others, but because there were many misunderstandings about Jesus that needed balancing and clarifying. Getting our arms around the truth about the life and identity of Jesus is important for the church, and it's just as important to our study of miracles.

C. S. Lewis puts it this way:

> The central miracle asserted by Christians is the Incarnation. They say that God became Man. Every other miracle prepares for this, or exhibits this, or results from this. . . . The fitness, and therefore credibility, of the particular miracles depends on their relation to the Grand Miracle; all discussion of them in isolation from it is futile.[5]

The Grand Miracle. I like that phrase. The Grand Miracle is that God became flesh and lived among us. The "particular miracles" that Jesus does, as Lewis calls them, are all meant to point to the Grand Miracle that is Jesus.

Let's recall a few of the "particular miracles" we've been studying together in light of the Grand Miracle of Jesus Himself.

Think back to the miracle of Jesus feeding the crowd of five thousand people. When the people from that crowd woke up the next morning, do you think they were hungry again? Of course they were!

How about the people who drank the wine at the wedding at Cana? Did they ever get thirsty again? I'm sure they did.

The seas that Jesus calmed were at some later point stirred up again by a storm. The sick people who Jesus healed probably suffered some kind of sickness again in their lives.

Jesus even warned that driving out demons isn't necessarily permanent, that the demon could return and bring friends along when it did (see Matthew 12:43-45).

Finally, think of the people who Jesus raised from the dead: Lazarus, Jairus's daughter, and the son of the widow of Nain. They were miraculously alive again, but at some point, whether soon after their encounter with Jesus or much later in life, all of them died again.

None of the particular miracles is permanent. Each fades away. But all point to Jesus and to the Grand Miracle of who He is, which is permanent. All other miracles exist to point us to relationship with the One who *is* our miracle. Once we have Him, neither hunger nor thirst nor sickness nor even death can separate us from Him (Romans 8:38-39).

> **All other miracles exist to point us to relationship with the One who *is* our miracle.**

Even as Jesus' impending birth was announced to his mother, Mary, the angel told her that "of his kingdom there will be no end" (Luke 1:33). Jesus is the miracle that will never run out. The fact that He *is* will always be enough.

Here's a hard but beautiful reality for those of us who pray for miracles but sometimes seem to come up empty-handed: if desperation drives us to Jesus, asking for help, then we have received the greatest miracle of all—the one that will never fade or fail. Have you opened your heart and hands to ask Jesus to fill your needs with Himself today? If you have, He will never disappoint.

I want to offer you these beautiful words that have deeply moved me, written by the ancient theologian and church father Augustine in the fourth century about the mystery of the Incarnation:

> Man's maker was made man that He, Ruler of the stars, might nurse at
> His mother's breast; that the Bread might hunger, the Fountain thirst,
> the Light sleep, the Way be tired on its journey; that Truth might be
> accused of false witnesses, the Teacher be beaten with whips, the
> Foundation be suspended on wood; that Strength might grow weak;
> that the Healer might be wounded; that Life might die.[6]

Jesus is our miracle of miracles. The God of the universe knows our name, our pain, and our desperation.

What do you find most beautiful about the Grand Miracle that is Jesus Himself?

What do you find most confusing or mysterious about the Grand Miracle that is Jesus Himself?

God bent low to become one of us and pave a road back to Him.

We've read the stories of the miracles Jesus performed, but the greatest—the grandest—miracle of all is that God bent low to become one of us and pave a road back to Him. Tomorrow we'll consider just how low God would bend to know us. For now, end your study time by reflecting on the miracle stories you've studied in the last few weeks and asking how they point you to Jesus Himself. Meditate on Jesus as your very own miracle. When we invite Jesus to be the Lord of our lives, we walk right into a miracle story of our own.

Talk with God

Jesus, You are a miracle. When I get frustrated waiting for You to act, remind me that You have already overcome death. When I'm praying for a particular miracle, remind me that You are the Grand Miracle. You came down to rescue and restore us. You came down to make a way to live with You in a burden-free, tear-free eternity. Fill me with hope today and give me an opportunity to speak hope to someone else. Amen.

DAY 2: THE MIRACLE OF GOD BENT LOW

Read God's Word

⁵Let the same mind be in you that was in Christ Jesus,

> *⁶who, though he was in the form of God,*
> *did not regard equality with God*
> *as something to be exploited,*
> *⁷but emptied himself,*
> *taking the form of a slave,*
> *being born in human likeness.*

And being found in human form,
     ⁸he humbled himself
     and became obedient to the point of death—
     even death on a cross.

⁹Therefore God also highly exalted him
     and gave him the name
     that is above every name,
¹⁰so that at the name of Jesus
     every knee should bend,
     in heaven and on earth and under the earth,
¹¹and every tongue should confess
     that Jesus Christ is Lord,
     to the glory of God the Father.
                   (Philippians 2:5-11)

⁴Joseph also went from the town of Nazareth in Galilee to Judea, to the city of David called Bethlehem, because he was descended from the house and family of David. ⁵He went to be registered with Mary, to whom he was engaged and who was expecting a child. ⁶While they were there, the time came for her to deliver her child. ⁷And she gave birth to her firstborn son and wrapped him in bands of cloth, and laid him in a manger, because there was no place for them in the inn.

⁸In that region there were shepherds living in the fields, keeping watch over their flock by night. ⁹Then an angel of the Lord stood before them, and the glory of the Lord shone around them, and they were terrified. ¹⁰But the angel said to them, "Do not be afraid; for see—I am bringing you good news of great joy for all the people: ¹¹to you is born this day in the city of David a Savior, who is the Messiah, the Lord. ¹²This will be a sign for you: you will find a child wrapped in bands of cloth and lying in a manger."

                   (Luke 2:4-12)

Reflect and Respond

The weeks leading up to Christmas are always a season of expectation and preparation. It's certainly true in my house as I'm sure it is in yours. We look forward to gatherings, plan for parties, shop for gifts, and decorate as if our lives depended on it! With all the emphasis on preparation, I sometimes start to believe that Christmas depends on me. I catch myself thinking that if I will just do all the right things ahead of time, Christmas will turn out perfectly. Have you ever had similar thoughts?

Sometimes, no matter how much we prepare, Christmas turns out differently than we expected.

I've heard stories of families whose oven broke while the turkey was cooking, and they had to drive around and look for somewhere they could get takeout. Or I think about the family that had everything planned to a T, except the mom went into early labor just before the Christmas Eve celebration and delivered a Christmas surprise. I've listened to plenty of families tell about lean Christmases when they had so little money for gifts and celebration that they thought it would be the worst Christmas ever, but it turned out to be one of their best.

Sometimes the unexpected brings more sobering memories, such as Christmases when grief is the unwanted companion because there's an empty seat at the table. Or a conflict in the family makes conversations tense and relationships strained. Or sometimes the greatest wish of a heart remains unfulfilled because it's not anything that can be put under a tree.

When and how has Christmas turned out differently than you expected?

What happens when Christmas throws us a curveball? What does it mean when our celebrations aren't perfect but are messy, unexpected, and surprising in all the wrong ways?

We need to keep in mind that Christmas was a miracle precisely *because* it was unexpected. God's people had been waiting for a Messiah to come for so long that they had gotten their hopes up very high. They imagined great things about the Messiah: that he would be strong and powerful, a commanding political leader as the world had never known. When they anticipated his birth, they knew that a mighty king, of course, would be born in a palace, wrapped in the finest cloths, and placed in a fancy bed.

But that's certainly not what the Messiah's first visitors found. They found a poor family in a borrowed space intended for animals. Max Lucado paints it this way: "Majesty in the midst of the mundane. Holiness in the filth of sheep manure and sweat. Divinity entering the world on the floor of a stable, through the womb of a teenager and in the presence of a carpenter."[7]

Make two lists below. In the left column, list some of the grandest ways you can think of for God to enter the world. Include details about things such as location, surroundings, visitors, and anything else that would communicate high status.

Now reread Luke 2:4-12. In the right column, list the actual way God entered the world in human flesh, including details about all of the same categories.

A Grand Entrance	God's Actual Entrance

If the shepherds had come with assumptions about how a king should enter the world, they might have rejected the simple baby they found lying in an animal's feeding trough and wrapped in rags. The thing is, the shepherds were the lowliest class of people around. If something was stolen from your home or property in those days, you might look warily and with suspicion on a group of shepherds passing through. Shepherds were the unlikely first visitors of an unlikely newborn King.

The miracle of Incarnation, of God uniting with human flesh, is an act of divine condescension. Normally we think of the word *condescending* as a negative word, as in someone speaking in a condescending way, patronizingly letting you know he or she is lowering themselves to your level. But according to Merriam-Webster, the most basic definition includes no negativity (see Extra Insight). The root word *con* means "together," and *descend* means "to come down." God's condescension simply means that He came down so we could be together. It means that He bent to our level, that He stooped low from the thing that made Him God and took on the things that make us human.

One scholar puts it this way:

> If there is going to be a corporate merger between a divine being and a human nature, then the divine side of the equation must necessarily limit itself, take on certain limitations, in order to be truly and fully human. The next question is . . . what does it mean to be fully human? It means to have limitations of time and space and knowledge and power, and of course being mortal. Jesus exhibited all these traits.[8]

Extra Insight

Condescension – "voluntary descent from one's rank or dignity in relations with an inferior."[9]

Read Philippians 2:5-11 and answer the following questions.

What is Jesus' nature? (v. 6)

What did He refuse to use to His advantage? (v. 6)

What nature did He take on? (v. 7)

How did He humble Himself? (v. 8)

In order to be with us, God limited Himself—the Creator stooped to meet the level of creation. But He didn't stop there! God didn't become a human with high status or wealth or power; He became *powerless*: "He made himself nothing by taking the very nature of a servant" (Philippians 2:7 NIV). Think of it: the Creator and Master of all things became a servant! That was the person of lowest status in society.

It has been said that "Jesus became the lowest of the low, to show us that no one was beneath his dignity, that every human was worth saving, was of sacred worth."[10] The idea of Jesus' lowliness bringing Him to recognize the dignity and worth of even the lowliest human brings us back to the particular miracles, the ones we've been studying for the last six weeks together. If the Grand Miracle of the Incarnation means that every person matters to Jesus—especially those who are in dire and desperate need—then we can see this work itself out in the miracles He performs.

Look again at the miracles of Jesus in the following Scriptures, and answer two questions for each:

1.) How did Jesus bend to the level of the person in need of a miracle?

2.) How would an observer be surprised that Jesus chose this particular individual for a miracle?

Matthew 8:1-3

1.

2.

Matthew 15:21-28

1.

2.

Can you think of other miracles where Jesus reached out to the lowly? If so, name them below:

Read the Scriptures below. What happened when someone who was not seeking a miracle out of humble need demanded a miracle from Jesus?

Matthew 12:38-39

Luke 23:8-9

When we look at miracles through this lens, we see that the desperate receive help, the downtrodden are lifted up, and the untouchable feel a touch from Jesus. However, those who approach Jesus in pride and entitlement have not yet stooped to the level to meet the God who has stooped to meet them.

Dietrich Bonheoffer, a German pastor and theologian who was imprisoned and murdered by the Nazis in World War II, makes an incredible statement about the connection between God and the lowly:

> Only the humble believe him and rejoice that God is so free and so marvelous that he does wonders where people despair, that he takes what is little and lowly and makes it marvelous. And that is the wonder of all wonders, that God loves the lowly.... God is not ashamed of the lowliness of human beings. God marches right in. He chooses people as his instruments and performs his wonders where one would

Those who approach Jesus in pride and entitlement have not yet stooped to the level to meet the God who has stooped to meet them.

least expect them. God is near to lowliness; he loves the lost, the neglected, the unseemly, the excluded, the weak and broken.[11]

Let that sink in: "He does wonders where people despair." Desperation precedes a miracle. Not only the "particular miracles" we've seen Jesus offer one by one to people in need but also the Grand Miracle of the Incarnation— the miracle offered to each and every one of us. God's people, His beloved children, were in a state of despair and desperation, and He moved heaven and earth in order to bend low to be with us. He gave everything, even Himself, to buy our ransom and accomplish our rescue.

Sometimes people talk about being in "incarnational ministry." By this they usually mean that they are somehow moving closer to people they want to minister to and entering their world in order to share Christ with them. I want to invite you to think about ways you are being called to display the same kind of love Jesus did that we read about earlier in Philippians 2:5-11. He put His own needs, status, and preferences on a back-burner in order to come close to us. Paul invites us to enter into this way of being: "In your relationships with one another, have the same mindset as Christ Jesus" (Philippians 2:5 NIV).

What does it mean to have the "same mindset as Christ Jesus" in your interactions with others?

Do you find humility an easy or difficult task? How can looking to Jesus help you find some freedom to put others higher than yourself?

Who can you come close to today on her or his own terms?

> **The Incarnation isn't just about Christmas; it's about every moment when we find ourselves in deep need of a savior.**

The Incarnation isn't just about Christmas; it's about every moment when we find ourselves in deep need of a savior. But it does make me think again of that first Christmas morning with the animals around the manger. Whatever season it may be as you are reading this, I hope that preparation will begin in your heart for a perfect Christmas next time December rolls around. Not the kind of perfect achieved with the perfectly decorated house and the perfectly wrapped presents, but the perfectly humbled heart prepared to receive a God who would stoop so low that a young woman would scoop Him to her breast and hold Him tight.

"We were all looking for a king to slay our foes and lift us high, but thou camst a little baby thing, that made a mother cry."[12]

I pray that this heart attitude will be yours every day of the year, reminding you that Jesus stooped low so that He could lift you up.

Talk with God

God, thank You for stooping to meet me where I am. Your love and mercy are overwhelming. It's hard to believe that You love us all so much that You came here to live as one of us, to know us, to save us, and to make a way to be with us forever. When I think too highly of myself, God, remind me that Jesus Himself didn't see equality with You as something to be used to His advantage. Remind me that Jesus humbled Himself for my sake. Help me to humble myself to be like Him. Amen.

DAY 3: THE MIRACLE OF CREATION RAISED UP

Read God's Word

For you know the generous act of our Lord Jesus Christ, that though he was rich, yet for your sakes he became poor, so that by his poverty you might become rich.

(2 Corinthians 8:9)

[12]*Therefore, just as sin came into the world through one man, and death came through sin, and so death spread to all because all have sinned—*[13]*sin was indeed in the world before the law, but sin is not reckoned when there is no law.* [14]*Yet death exercised dominion from Adam to Moses, even over those whose sins were not like the transgression of Adam, who is a type of the one who was to come.*

[15]*But the free gift is not like the trespass. For if the many died through the one man's trespass, much more surely have the grace of God and the free gift in the grace of the one man, Jesus Christ, abounded for the many.* [16]*And the free gift is not like the effect of the one man's sin. For the judgment following one trespass brought condemnation, but the free gift following many trespasses brings justification.* [17]*If, because of the one man's trespass, death exercised dominion through that one, much more surely will those who receive the abundance of grace and the free gift of righteousness exercise dominion in life through the one man, Jesus Christ.*

[18]*Therefore just as one man's trespass led to condemnation for all, so one man's act of righteousness leads to justification and life for all.* [19]*For just as by the one*

man's disobedience the many were made sinners, so by the one man's obedience the
many will be made righteous. ²⁰But law came in, with the result that the trespass
multiplied; but where sin increased, grace abounded all the more, ²¹so that, just
as sin exercised dominion in death, so grace might also exercise dominion through
justification leading to eternal life through Jesus Christ our Lord.

(Romans 5:12-21)

Reflect and Respond

I'm a crier. I cry mostly in happy moments, such as when I see something remarkable in my children's faces or when I'm overwhelmed by the blessings in my life that I've done nothing to deserve. I cry in church a lot, but I also cry in movies, at the happy endings of books, and when someone shares good news with me. One day my daughter was crying, and I explained that mommy cries sometimes too. She was curious, since she doesn't usually see me fall down and hurt myself or wake up scared in the night—her usual reasons for crying. As I told her about some of the reasons I cry, she exclaimed, "Oh! You cry for goodness!"

Sometimes I cry when I read the Bible to my children. It's such an overwhelming feeling to introduce them to stories that have meant so much to me, stories of God's great truth that will bless their lives more than they can know. Usually this is the kind of crying where my voice will start to crack and then stop working altogether. And my son will turn around and ask, "Mommy, are you crying *again*?"

One night it happened as we were reading the story of the Fall in their children's Bible, retold from the account in Genesis 3. As Adam and Eve broke God's rule and ate the fruit they shouldn't, what might have been an unhappy ending to this particular story ended with a promise of God's forever love and longing for them—and their longing for Him and the home He had created:

> You see no matter what, in spite of everything, God would love his
> children—with a Never Stopping, Never Giving Up, Unbreaking,
> Always and Forever Love.

> And though they would forget him, and run from him, deep in their
> hearts God's children would miss him always, and long for him—lost
> children yearning for their home.[13]

As I read that part, my voice just about stopped altogether. I was crying for goodness again.

In the Grand Miracle of God coming to earth in human flesh, the Incarnation, we witness the "Never Stopping, Never Giving Up, Unbreaking, Always and Forever Love" of God in its ultimate form. God is pursuer, rescuer, savior. Some people don't realize that the Incarnation was not the beginning of God's rescue plan in Jesus but the culmination. This plan had been unfolding long before God walked with human feet on creation.

One reason the Incarnation is not the beginning of God's rescue plan is that God had been pursuing His children throughout history. He called to them of His love through every possible means, both pleasing and difficult, for humanity to receive. God's self-giving love had been chasing after His people ever since that moment He searched out His shame-filled and hiding children in the garden, calling out "Where are you?" with the voice of a concerned parent hunting a lost child.

Another reason the Incarnation is not the beginning of God's rescue plan is that it's not Jesus' beginning—only His debut. What do I mean by that? Jesus, as a part of the Trinity—the one-God-in-three-persons Father, Son, and Holy Spirit—is eternal: without beginning or end. Before any human person could see Him, there had always been a divine Son of God, even before He became a human being.

Read Colossians 1:15-17 in the margin. Where was Jesus when the creation of the world happened?

[15]He is the image of the invisible God, the firstborn of all creation; [16]for in him all things in heaven and on earth were created, things visible and invisible, whether thrones or dominions or rulers or powers—all things have been created through him and for him. [17]He himself is before all things, and in him all things hold together.

(Colossians 1:15-17)

So the Son was present even before the world was created, and the moment He united with human flesh to become 100 percent God and 100 percent human was simply His visible debut on earth, an earth that He created. Yesterday we pondered how this unification of God and human flesh meant God had to become low. Today we'll see that God not only stooped down in this union; we'll also see the miracle of how He raises up creation itself.

Let's explore four miracles clustered together in this "raising up."

1. The miracle of our sins forgiven

God's Grand Miracle in human flesh made a way for our sins to be forgiven in Jesus' sacrifice for us. When Jesus became human, He did something no human had ever done. He did not sin. This helps us understand God's original design for humans—a life without sin—and to see that God wants us to confess our own sins and find forgiveness in Him.

Our Scripture for today's lesson compares the sin of Adam (the first human) and the perfect forgiveness found in Jesus (God made human).

Reread Romans 5:12-21 and answer the following questions:

How did sin enter the world? How did death enter the world? (v. 12)

How did the gift of grace enter the world? (v. 15)

Refer to verses 16-21 to complete the following chart.

Results of Adam's Actions	Results of Jesus' Actions

Here is the Grand Miracle of our sins forgiven in Jesus: because sin came from a human, only a human could offer a sacrifice that could satisfy the cost of sin—which, according to Romans 3:23, is death. But at the same time, only

God was able to undo the curse brought on by Adam and Eve's sin and seen in every human life since. So, only One who was both human and God could make this miracle of sin forgiven a reality for us.

2. The miracle of our adoption as heirs

The Grand Miracle of the Incarnation not only means our sins are forgiven; it also means an end to our alienation from God and our adoption into His family.

Look up Galatians 4:4-7, and complete these statements based on the truths you find there:

I am no longer a _____. I am God's

_____. And since I am His _____,

God also has made me an _____.

How does it feel to know that you are God's child and heir? Look back at the "particular miracle" on Week 5, Day 2 (page 147). Remember how Jairus felt about his cherished only daughter? Remember how Jesus felt about the woman who was healed? This is how God feels about *you*, His daughter!

When God looks at you, what does He see? To answer this, imagine God looking at you through the lens of a loving parent looking at a cherished daughter. Write words below to describe what He sees:

God lowers Himself so that He can raise us up to become unified with Him, to become part of His family.

3. The miracle of the blessing of humankind

The Grand Miracle of the Incarnation means a deep blessing on what it means to be human. Because God chose to unite God and humanity in Jesus Christ, who we are is forever bound up with who God is. It forever changes how we see ourselves and our relationship with God.

> The Grand Miracle of the Incarnation not only means our sins are forgiven; it also means an end to our alienation from God and our adoption into His family.

Extra Insight

"The Son of God became man to enable men to become the sons of God."

–C. S. Lewis[14]

For you know the generous act of our Lord Jesus Christ, that though he was rich, yet for your sakes he became poor, so that by his poverty you might become rich.

(2 Corinthians 8:9)

Read 2 Corinthians 8:9 in the margin. What is the exchange of riches between Jesus and humankind? What kinds of riches do you think this passage refers to?

Jason Byassee writes, "When God becomes human we can no longer think of God or humanity the same way. God is forever one person. All persons are now forever tinged with the divine. Everything that is ever good, holy, or beautiful in any human being who has ever lived is already a reflection of the goodness, holiness, and beauty of God."[15]

Whenever we see another person, we can know that God loved him or her enough to become like him or her. This changes our capacity to love that person as well—and to love the human we see in the mirror!

4. *The miracle of creation restored*

The Incarnation gives us a new lens of love through which to see ourselves and other human beings, since God united with the flesh of humanity in Jesus Christ. But God doesn't stop there! Jesus is not only human; He is a part of creation.

When sin entered the world, Adam and Eve and our human family were not the only ones damaged. The entire creation was reduced from its original state to a now-damaged existence.

One of my favorite Advent carols, "Joy to the World," talks about the restoration of all of creation to its original dignity and blessing through the birth of Jesus:

No more let sins and sorrows grow,
   nor thorns infest the ground;
he comes to make his blessings flow
     far as the curse is found.[16]

The Incarnation affirms our role and obligation to care for a creation that God did not abandon but united with in flesh.

In Jesus, God unites with His creation in a way that says He has not abandoned it but is committed to its full restoration. The Incarnation shows that it is right to delight in creation, because God delights in creation. The Incarnation shows why Christians have been leaders in the arts, sciences, and all fields of knowledge that explore creation. The Incarnation affirms our role and obligation to care for a creation that God did not abandon but united with in flesh.

The Synod of Alexandria, held in AD 360, stated that "only that which God becomes is healed."[17] The good news is that God united with creation, so all of His creation will be healed in the coming of His kingdom.

Stop for a moment to think of the miracles of Jesus we have been studying together. In them, God does not offer simply spiritual, invisible blessing. He touches the stuff of earth and makes it healed and whole. He multiplies bread, gives sight to blind eyes, walks on water, and touches lepers. These are tangible parts of creation that God calls "good" just as in the first days of Creation. But now He blesses His creation by uniting His own Son with the earth that He made and loves.

I hope the reality of God's love for His world gives you new eyes to see and new love for a world on which God bestowed a deep blessing by becoming flesh. Praise God: the Creator stooped to become creature in order to restore His creation. And He did that for you and for me!

Talk with God

God, You have given us a tinge of the divine. Thank You for loving us so much and for bringing Your healing and wholeness to our sin-sick and broken hearts. You have blessed Your creation by sending Your own Son as our Rescuer. Give me eyes of wonder as I see the world that You have made. Give me eyes of wonder as I read Your Word. Give me eyes of wonder as I remember Your never-stopping, never-giving-up love for me. Amen.

DAY 4: INCARNATION FULFILLED

Read God's Word

45From noon on, darkness came over the whole land until three in the afternoon. 46And about three o'clock Jesus cried with a loud voice, "Eli, Eli, lema sabachthani?" that is, "My God, my God, why have you forsaken me?" 47When some of the bystanders heard it, they said, "This man is calling for Elijah." 48At once one of them ran and got a sponge, filled it with sour wine, put it on a stick, and gave it to him to drink. 49But the others said, "Wait, let us see whether Elijah will come to save him." 50Then Jesus cried again with a loud voice and breathed his last. 51At that moment the curtain of the temple was torn in two, from top to bottom. The earth shook, and the rocks were split. 52The tombs also were opened, and many bodies of the saints who had fallen asleep were raised. 53After his resurrection they came out of the tombs and entered the holy city and appeared to many. 54Now when the centurion and those with him, who were keeping watch over Jesus, saw the earthquake and what took place, they were terrified and said, "Truly this man was God's Son!"

(Matthew 27:45-54)

Reflect and Respond

I've been reading C. S. Lewis's fantasy series *The Chronicles of Narnia* aloud to my seven-year-old son, Drew. I've been an avid reader since I was his age, but I'm not sure I've ever experienced such great joy in reading as I do when I share with him a book I have treasured, and the Narnia series is absolutely one of my favorites. On one level, this series is about an imaginary world called Narnia, where animals talk, battles are fought, and magical spells are made and broken. For Drew, the adventure story is just that: a story well told with heroes and action that keep him wanting more in each chapter. To him, the lion called Aslan is a strong and valiant king of the realm, a huge lion who captures his imagination. But to me the story is so much more, because C. S. Lewis wrote Aslan as an illustration of Jesus: strong and valiant but also forgiving and humble, willing to sacrifice His own life for children even when they act their worst.

Remember yesterday when I confessed that I'm a crier? What is it about reading to my kids that leaves me in a puddle of tears each night? Well, my Drew has started to notice that when I read the parts about Aslan, I almost always start crying. I will be reading along and suddenly my eyes well up with tears and my voice gets all funny. Drew will look over the edge of the book at me and ask, "Mom . . . are you crying *again*?"

It's funny how easily the stories about Aslan can make me cry! He is, in a way, an incarnational figure that represents Jesus' character so well that I can't help but getting emotional in the moments in the story when he appears—not only because the fictional story is so good but also because The Story behind it is true, has saved me, and is the best and most beautiful story I know.

In *The Lion, the Witch, and the Wardrobe*, Aslan actually lays down his life for the most treacherous of the children. When the child has betrayed his own family and friends, the witch of the story reminds them that she is owed the traitor's blood. Aslan makes a deal with her that she can have his blood in exchange and then goes willingly with her as he is tied down, his magnificent mane is shaved, and then he is killed. I'm not sure how I made it through that part of the story, but I cried all the way! The truth of Jesus laying down His life for us was just too overwhelming, moving me in a whole new way as I read aloud to my son, who I hope will someday understand what it means that Jesus died for him.

We've been talking this week about the Grand Miracle of Jesus' incarnation, and we've seen that the greatest miracle of all is who Jesus is. We've also seen that every other miracle flows from that reality. These other "particular miracles" are signs that point us to Jesus Himself, our only permanent gift. Today I want us to think specifically about Jesus' death and resurrection and how these events were really the fulfillment of His incarnation.

> "Particular miracles" are signs that point us to Jesus Himself, our only permanent gift.

What do I mean by that? Well, for Jesus to be fully human, He had to experience the full range of human experience, which for every human being who has ever lived has meant death. As someone once put it: no matter how science advances, the death rate is 100 percent—it never goes up or down! So, for Jesus to be fully human, He had to die.

Read 1 Corinthians 1:23-25 in the margin. How might the crucifixion of Jesus be seen as weakness and foolisÚess?

How might it be seen as wisdom and strength?

[23]We proclaim Christ crucified, a stumbling block to Jews and foolisÚess to Gentiles, [24]but to those who are the called, both Jews and Greeks, Christ the power of God and the wisdom of God. [25]For God's foolisÚess is wiser than human wisdom, and God's weakness is stronger than human strength.
(1 Corinthians 1:23-25)

You may have spent some time reflecting on the incarnation of Jesus before this study. We talk about it a lot right around Christmas when we celebrate His birth. And you've likely spent some time thinking about His death and resurrection, maybe around the Easter season when we celebrate and tell that story. But the connection between Christmas and Easter, between birth and death and resurrection, is an undeniable one.

For Jesus to be truly human, He had to die. For Jesus to defeat death, He had to be divine. The realization of Jesus as 100 percent human and 100 percent God is fully realized in His death and resurrection.

In the previous two days of our study, we've seen that the Incarnation means for God to be brought low and for creation to be raised up. Jesus' death and resurrection are the ultimate vision of these two steps—one deeply downward and the other sharply upward.

Where did you first learn about Jesus' death on the cross? What are your first memories of this story?

Even in His death Jesus identified with the greatest suffering and injustice of the world. Instead of a quick or painless death, Jesus' death would mean no one could claim He was immune to any kind of human sorrow.

One author notes, "On the cross Jesus suffered injustice, felt the shame of nakedness, was deprived of his rights, endured taunting, became the focus of

There is no human desperation that Jesus does not understand.

the rage of others, and was rejected and forsaken. In addition, he experienced excruciating physical pain, thirst, hunger, emptiness, torment, confusion and finally even death itself."[18] What does this mean for us? It means there is no human desperation that Jesus does not understand. In His lifetime Jesus showed an incredible compassion for the poor, the outcast, the grieving, the sick, the helpless, and the hopeless. What He lived in His life is impossible to ignore in His death as He hung between two thieves: Jesus would go to the lowest possible place to bring us to God.

Reflect on the miracle that there is nothing about your desperate moments that Jesus does not understand. Write your feelings below:

The prophet Isaiah named the purpose of Jesus' suffering for us well, relating His suffering to our healing:

4Surely he has borne our infirmities
   and carried our diseases;
yet we accounted him stricken,
   struck down by God, and afflicted.
5But he was wounded for our transgressions,
   crushed for our iniquities;
upon him was the punishment that made us whole,
   and by his bruises we are healed.

(Isaiah 53:4-5)

What does God do with our suffering? He doesn't ignore it; He joins us in it and transforms it to save the world. In his book *Give Them Christ*, Stephen Seamands writes, "God's solution to the problem of suffering is not to eliminate it, nor to insulate himself from it, but to participate in it, and having participated in it, to transform it into his instrument for redeeming the world."[19]

Reread Matthew 27:51. In what direction was the curtain of the temple ripped?

Does that imply a human act or an act of God, and why?

At the moment of Jesus' death, the curtain in the temple was ripped in two from top to bottom. This curtain divided the holy place from the most holy place or Holy of Holies, where God's presence was thought to live; and its tearing from top to bottom communicated that because Jesus had taken our sins and our punishment on Himself in His death, no division would ever need to exist again between God and His people.

Three days later when Jesus rose from the dead, another opening was created—the opening of the door of death that had locked humanity behind it since the day humans were exiled from the garden of Eden. C. S. Lewis puts it this way: "He has forced open a door that has been locked since the death of the first man. He has met, fought, and beaten the King of Death. Everything is different because He has done so. This is the beginning of the New Creation: a new chapter in cosmic history has opened."[20]

The ultimate understanding of Jesus' identity came at the moment of His crucifixion and His resurrection:

"Truly this man was God's Son!"
          (Matthew 27:54)

He was shown to be the Son of God when he was raised from the dead by the power of the Holy Spirit. He is Jesus Christ our Lord.

                                        (Romans 1:4 NLT)

So Jesus' death meant that He experienced the worst of human experience; that He had walked our earth, experienced our pain, and died our death. But His resurrection from the dead meant that the human experience would not have to end there. This miracle of Jesus' resurrection meant that we would be offered resurrection as well.

Read Romans 10:9 in the margin. What is the core thing we must declare and believe to be saved?

If you confess with your lips that Jesus is Lord and believe in your heart that God raised him from the dead, you will be saved. (Romans 10:9)

Reading my son C. S. Lewis's books about Narnia somehow made me weep over the death and resurrection in ways I hadn't done in years. The great lion Aslan had given his life for a traitor when he didn't deserve death. Two young girls had witnessed that death and then were the first to meet the resurrected Aslan—just like the women at the garden tomb who met Jesus. Here are the lines I read through tears to my son:

> "Oh, you're real, you're real! Oh, Aslan!" cried Lucy and both girls flung themselves upon him and covered him with kisses.
>
> "But what does it all mean?" asked Susan when they were somewhat calmer.
>
> "It means," said Aslan, "that though the Witch knew the Deep Magic, there is a magic deeper still which she did not know. Her knowledge goes back only to the dawn of Time. But if she could have looked a little further back, into the stillness and the darkness before Time dawned, she would have read there a different incantation. She would have known that when a willing victim who has committed no treachery was killed in a traitor's stead, the Table would crack and Death itself would start working backwards. And now—"
>
> "Oh yes. Now?" said Lucy jumping up and clapping her hands. . . .
>
> And now," said Aslan presently, "to business. I feel I am going to roar."[21]

Does that move you as it does me? The beauty of the Grand Miracle of Jesus is only a complete picture when we see His life, death, and resurrection as the way that He showed up for a desperate world and gave everything, holding nothing back—even His own life. I hope that today you've seen in new ways what this amazing gift means for *you*!

Talk with God

Jesus, I believe in my heart and confess with my mouth that You are the Lord. You are the God of the universe and the Savior of the world. You are the Rescuer, the Son of God, the Victor over the curse of sin and darkness. So I give my life to You again and again. I will follow You wherever you lead. Amen.

DAY 5: MIRACLE OF MIRACLES

Read God's Word

[15]For this reason, ever since I heard about your faith in the Lord Jesus and your love for all God's people, [16]I have not stopped giving thanks for you, remembering you in my prayers. [17]I keep asking that the God of our Lord Jesus Christ, the glorious Father, may give you the Spirit of wisdom and revelation, so that you may know

him better. [18]I pray that the eyes of your heart may be enlightened in order that you may know the hope to which he has called you, the riches of his glorious inheritance in his holy people, [19]and his incomparably great power for us who believe. That power is the same as the mighty strength [20]he exerted when he raised Christ from the dead and seated him at his right hand in the heavenly realms, [21]far above all rule and authority, power and dominion, and every name that is invoked, not only in the present age but also in the one to come. [22]And God placed all things under his feet and appointed him to be head over everything for the church, [23]which is his body, the fullness of him who fills everything in every way. (Ephesians 1:15-23 NIV)

Reflect and Respond

We made it! We've arrived at the last day of our study together. I hope that during the past weeks you have been encouraged, have grown in wisdom, and have felt connected to God and others.

For six weeks we've stood in awe looking into the beautiful person and work of Jesus as He walked the earth. In some ways it has been like standing on the edge of the Grand Canyon and gazing into its beauty. There are so many layers and colors that draw our attention—just like the individual and amazing miracles Jesus performed; but ultimately we stand back and have our breath taken away at the overall glory of the whole scene. This is where we've ended, being able to see the person of Jesus for the Grand Miracle that He is, not just the particular miracles that He does.

What miracle were you most familiar with before we began our study together?

What miracle were you least familiar with before we started?

If you could ask Jesus any question about miracles, what would it be?

Is there a person in one of the miracle stories that you identified with more than others? Why?

What miracle story is your favorite and why?

Throughout these weeks together we've learned that God is more compassionate and more powerful than we ever even imagined. In the well-known hymn "Holy, Holy, Holy," Reginald Heber writes these words of awe for the character of God:

Holy, holy, holy! Lord God Almighty!
Early in the morning our song shall rise to thee.
Holy, holy, holy! Merciful and mighty,
God in three persons, blessed Trinity![22]

> **Jesus will stop at nothing until all of His creation is restored, and nothing can stand in His way.**

Merciful and mighty. These two characteristics are bound up in the miracles of Jesus. His mercy causes Him to respond to the needs of those He loves. While others see desperation and are repelled by it, Jesus is drawn to desperation. His mercy means that He longs to help those who recognize their need for Him. His might means that there is no obstacle so great that He cannot overcome it. Jesus will stop at nothing until all of His creation is restored, and nothing can stand in His way.

Here's the beauty of Jesus combining the two: mercy without might would just be powerless sympathy, and might without mercy would mean power unchecked by love and grace. Thank God that He is both merciful and mighty!

Now that you've spent these six weeks meditating on Jesus' mercy and might, how would you describe Him to someone who doesn't know Him? Write a couple of sentences here, introducing someone to Jesus as if He is a stranger who walks into a gathering:

Jesus, meet Jane, she's a friend of mine.
Jane, meet Jesus, He's . . .

We also connected with the other side of the miracle equation: those who needed the miracles, those who were desperate enough to turn to Jesus. In my own story, I can think of desperate moments when I've cried out to God because I knew I couldn't fix things myself.

Can you think of times in your life that you've needed and leaned on Jesus' mercy? Describe one of those times below:

Just remembering those moments can remind us of the closeness we felt to God when we realized we had nothing else to depend on but Him. Our desperate moments are touchstones we can look back on when we need to remember God's power is at work now.

Those moments of desperation where God was enough for us when nothing else was can bring the spirit of yesterday's desperation forward into today, keeping us in touch with the fact that although we desperately need God, we do not have to live desperate lives in order to receive this miracle of Jesus. He doesn't want our lives to be chaotic and crazy; He simply wants our hearts to be surrendered to Him. Having a desperate heart means that we remember we need Jesus on our best day as much as we did on our worst day.

In Paul's Letter to the Ephesians, he offers a prayer for this church he loves.

Reread Ephesians 1:18-20, and summarize Paul's prayer below:

The power Paul wants them to know and receive is the very same power that God exerted when He raised Christ from the dead. This is the power we've been dipping our toes into as we've walked together through the miracles of Jesus. The power that healed lepers, calmed storms, fed thousands, and met and answered the desperation of even the smallest and most undeserving person. What could it mean that this power is at work in those who believe? What a grand miracle, indeed, that the same power that raised Christ and defeated death is here surrounding you right now!

As our study draws to a close, take a moment to consider what this journey has meant to you.

Complete each of the following statements:

Something surprising I've learned from this study is . . .

> Our desperate moments are touchstones we can look back on when we need to remember God's power is at work now.

> Having a desperate heart means that we remember we need Jesus on our best day as much as we did on our worst day.

Something I've learned about myself is ...

Something I've learned about God is ...

Because of what I've learned, I want to live differently by ...

My prayer for you is that this study has given you an increased awareness of God's power—His merciful might that connects Him with our needs and the needs of His creation. I also hope that when you trip on your own powerlessness, you'll see it as a gift: a moment to turn your desperate heart to the God who hears and sees. And when you encounter needs in others, I hope you'll find an "incarnational" moment to come near to them in their pain the way Jesus has come near to you. I pray that from this day forward, you will know and remember that the greatest and most permanent miracle is Jesus Himself, the One who will never leave you or forsake you. He is your greatest hope and help. He is your miracle!

Talk with God

God of Miracles, thank You for this journey of discovering Your miracle-working power. Your might and mercy have been on display through the stories of Jesus walking this earth. Open the eyes of my heart to see Your miracles all around. Give me the courage to act or speak when You call me to participate in Your everyday miracles. May the same power that raised Jesus from the dead be the power that I seek not only when I'm desperate but also for each and every day. Amen.

VIDEO VIEWER GUIDE: WEEK 6

Every time we meet together as Christians, we're participating in a kind of miracle after The Miracle, _____.

Every gathering of believers in the Grand Miracle of Jesus is a reunion of the _____.

All other miracles exist to point us to _____ with the One who *is* our miracle.

Once we have Him, neither hunger nor thirst nor sickness nor even death can _____ us from Him.

Colossians 1:15-20

The Grand Miracle is that God would choose to come and _____ _____ us and _____ not only our best moments but also our hardest, most difficult ones.

God became desperate in order to _____ us from our desperation.

To become the rescued and transformed means to be those _____ on the rescue and transformation of _____.

VIDEO VIEWER GUIDE ANSWERS

Week 1
desperation

run out / Jesus

acknowledge

need / Jesus

power

small / big

Week 2
nothing / everything

Himself

bread / life

Week 3
distant / boat

dark

desperate / risk

Week 4
help

slow / imperceptible

blind / follow

see / treat

difficulties / participation

Week 5
gift

relationship

left out

death

Week 6
Jesus / rescued

relationship / separate

live among / occupy

rescue

intent / others

Notes

Week 1

1. https://www.merriam-webster.com/dictionary/immanent, accessed May 23, 2017.
2. https://www.merriam-webster.com/dictionary/transcendent, accessed June 5, 2017.
3. *The Dictionary of Jesus and the Gospels*, ed. Joel Green, Scot McKnight, and Howard Marshall (Downers Grove, IL: Intervarsity Press, 1992), 872, s.v. "miracles.".
4. Timothy Keller, *Encounters with Jesus: Unexpected Answers to Life's Biggest Questions* (New York: Penguin, 2013), 59.
5. Kamila Blessing, *Families of the Bible: A New Perspective* (Westport, CT: Praeger, 2010), 41.
6. Craig S. Keener, IVP *Bible Background Commentary: New Testament* (Downer's Grove, IL.: InterVarsity Press, 2014), 253.

Week 2

1. Stuart Briscoe, *Brave Enough to Follow: What Jesus Can Do When You Keep Your Eyes on Him* (Colorado Springs: NavPress, 2004), 76.
2. Mark Buchanan, *Your God Is Too Safe: Rediscovering the Wonder of a God You Can't Control* (Sisters, OR: Multnomah, 2001), 39.
3. Joseph Martin, *Jesus: A Pilgrimage* (SanFrancisco: HarperOne, 2016), 258.
4. Strong's 966, s.v. "Bethsaida," http://biblehub.com/greek/966.htm
5. Robert A. Spivey and D. Moody Smith, *Anatomy of the New Testament* (Englewood Cliffs, NJ: Simon and Schuster, 1995), 163–166.
6. s.v. "Gospels," *The Dictionary of Jesus and the Gospels*, 294.
7. Leon Morris, *The Gospel According to John in the New International Commentary on the New Testament* (Grand Rapids: Eerdmans, 1995), 305.
8. Buchanan, *Your God Is Too Safe: Rediscovering the Wonder of a God You Can't Control*, 38.
9. Arland J. Hultgren, *Commentary on Luke*, Workingpreacher.com, https://www.workingpreacher.org/preaching.aspx?commentary_id=506, accessed May 25, 2017.

Week 3

1. Todd Bolen, "*Jesus and the Sea of Galilee*," first posted in *Bible and Spade* Fall 2003 issue and reprinted on their site Bible Archaeology, http://www.biblearchaeology.org/post/2009/03/Jesus-and-the-Sea-of-Galilee.aspx#Article, accessed May 25, 2017.
2. James Boyce, Commentary on Mark 4:35-41, Workingpreacher.org, https://www.workingpreacher.org/preaching.aspx?commentary_id=2470, accessed May 25, 2017.
3. David E. Garland, NIV *Application Commentary: Mark* (Grand Rapids: Zondervan, 1996), 263.
4. Reginald Heber, "Holy, Holy, Holy, Lord God Almighty," *The United Methodist Hymnal* (Nashville: The United Methodist Publishing House, 1989), 64, stanza 2.
5. Garland, NIV *Application Commentary: Mark*, 263.
6. Morgan Linn, "*Experts from Israel, Great Lakes Compare Big Water*," in Capital News Service online edition, http://news.jrn.msu.edu/capitalnewsservice/2016/10/07/experts-from-israel-great-lakes-compare-big-water/, accessed May 25, 2017.
7. Sharon H. Ringe, *Working Preacher*, Commentary on Mark 4:35-41, https://www.workingpreacher.org/preaching.aspx?commentary_id=276, accessed May 25, 2017.
8. Scott Walker, *Footsteps of the Fisherman: With St. Peter on the Path of Discipleship* (Minneapolis: Augsburg Fortress, 2003), 35.
9. Dr. Frank Stagg quoted in Walker, *Footsteps of the Fisherman*, 37.

Week 4

1. Mark Pearson, *Christian Healing: A Practical and Comprehensive Guide* (Lake Mary, FL: Charisma House, 2004), 4.
2. Keener, *IVP Bible Background Commentary*, 33.
3. "A Service of Word and Table 1," *The United Methodist Hymnal*, 8.
4. Keener, *IVP Bible Background Commentary*, 193.
5. *Strong's Concordance* number 922, http://biblehub.com/greek/922.htm, accessed June 6, 2017.
6. *Strong's Concordance* number 5413, http://biblehub.com/greek/5413.htm, accessed May 26, 2017.
7. Ben Witherington, *The Gospel of Mark: A Socio-Rhetorical Commentary* (Grand Rapids: Eerdmans, 2001), 266.
8. Craig S. Keener, *IVP Bible Background Commentary*, 146.
9. Ibid., 147.
10. "Zoo in Copenhagen Exhibits New Primates (Fully Clothed)," *New York Times* online edition August 29, 1996, http://www.nytimes.com/1996/08/29/world/zoo-in-copenhagen-exhibits-new-primates-fully-clothed.html, accessed June 5, 2017.
11. Keener, *The Gospel of John: A Commentary*, vol. 1 (Peabody: Hendrickson, 2003), 636.

Week 5

1. Many of these points of similarity are found in Joseph R. Dongell, *The Gospel of Mark*, Onebook: The Biblical Journey (Franklin, TN: Seedbed, 2015), 91.
2. Ibid.
3. Ibid.
4. *Elliocott's Commentary for English Readers*, http://biblehub.com/commentaries/john/11-33.htm, accessed May 26, 2017.
5. Stephen Seamands in Theology and Practice of Healing class (TH 635) at Asbury Theological Seminary. Fall 2015.
6. Craig S. Keener, *Mark* 1:40–45.
7. Johannes P. Louw and Eugene Albert Nida, *Greek-English Lexicon of the New Testament: Based on Semantic Domains* (New York: United Bible Societies, 1996), 293.
8. Donald Demaray, *Experiencing Healing and Wholeness: A Journey in Faith* (Indianapolis: Light and Life Communications, 1999), 178–179.

Week 6

1. Ben Witherington, *The Meaning of Incarnation*, http://www.patheos.com/blogs/bibleandculture/2012/12/23/the-meaning-of-incarnation/, accessed May 27, 2017.
2. *Strong's Concordance* number 4637. Greek lexicon based on *Thayer's and Smith's Bible Dictionary*.
3. "The Apostles' Creed, Traditional Version," *The United Methodist Hymnal*, (Nashville: The United Methodist Publishing House, 1989), 881.
4. "The Apostles' Creed, Ecumenical Version," (Nashville: The United Methodist Publishing House, 1989), 882.
5. C. S. Lewis, *Miracles* (first published 1947; New York: HarperCollins, 2001), 173–174.
6. Augustine of Hippo, Sermons 191.1.
7. Max Lucado, *God Came Near* (Nashville: Thomas Nelson, 2002), 4.
8. Ben Witherington, *The Meaning of Incarnation*.
9. Merriam-Webster Collegiate Dictionary, s.v., "Condensation," https://www.merriam-webster.com/dictionary/condescension, accessed May 27, 2017.
10. Ben Witherington, *The Meaning of Incarnation*, accessed May 27, 2017.
11. Dietrich Bonhoeffer, *God Is in the Manger: Reflections on Advent and Christmas*, edited by Jana Riess (Louisville: Westminster John Knox Press, 2010), 22.
12. George MacDonald, quoted by Ben Witherington, *The Meaning of Incarnation*.

13. Sally Lloyd-Jones, *The Jesus Storybook Bible: Every Story Whispers His Name* (Grand Rapids: Zondervan, 2007), 36.

14. C. S. Lewis, *Mere Christianity* (San Francisco: HarperOne, 2015), 46.

15. Jason Byassee, *Trinity: The God We Don't Know* (Nashville: Abingdon Press, 2015), 74.

16. Isaac Watts, "Joy to the World," *The United Methodist Hymnal*, (Nashville: The United Methodist Publishing House, 1989), 246.

17. "The Synod of Alexandria," quoted by Robert E. Webber in *Ancient-Future Faith: Rethinking Evangelicalism for a Postmodern World* (Grand Rapids: Baker, 1999), 65.

18. Frank Lake, *Clinical Theology: A Theological and Psychiatric Basis to Clinical Pastoral Care* (London: Darton, Longman & Todd, 1966), 18.

19. Stephen Seamands, *Give Them Christ: Preaching His Incarnation, Crucifixion, Resurrection, Ascension and Return* (Downers Grove, IL: InterVarsity Press, 2015), 71.

20. C. S. Lewis, *Miracles*, 236–237.

21. C. S. Lewis, *The Lion, the Witch, and the Wardrobe* (New York: Collier, 1970), 159–160.

22. Heber, "Holy, Holy, Holy, Lord God Almighty," 64, stanza 1.

More from Jessica LaGrone

Bible Studies

Set Apart: Holy Habits of Prophets and Kings
Workbook ISBN: 9781426778421

Draw closer to God through spiritual practices.

Broken and Blessed: How God Used One Imperfect Family to Change the World
Workbook ISBN: 9781426778377

See how God brings blessings from our brokenness.

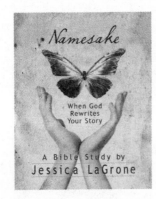

Namesake: When God Rewrites Your Story
Workbook ISBN: 9781426761874

Discover people in Scripture whose lives and names were changed forever by God.

Book

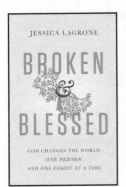

Broken & Blessed: God Changes the World One Person and One Family at a Time
Trade Book ISBN: 9781426774911

The first family in Genesis was a mess by anyone's standards but God chose them for His purpose just as God chooses each of us and our families today.

DVD, leader guide, and kit also available for each six-week study.

Discover samples of her book and Bible studies at AbingdonWomen.com/JessicaLaGrone

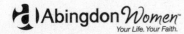

Available wherever books are sold.

More Women's Bible Studies From Abingdon Women
Your Life. Your Faith.

First Corinthians: Living Love When We Disagree
How to show love when we disagree without compromising our convictions.

Workbook ISBN: 9781501801686

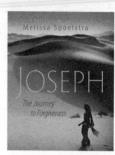

Joseph: The Journey to Forgiveness
Finding Freedom Through Forgiveness.

Workbook ISBN: 9781426789106

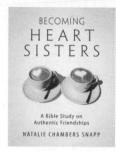

Becoming Heart Sisters: A Bible Study on Authentic Friendships
Explore the Bible and learn to cultivate God-honoring relationships.

Workbook ISBN: 9781501821202

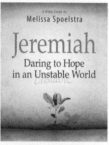

Jeremiah: Daring to Hope in an Unstable World
Learn to surrender to God's will and rest your hope in Him alone.

Workbook ISBN: 9781426788871

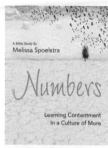

Numbers: Learning Contentment in a Culture of More
Say no to the desire for bigger, better, faster.

Workbook ISBN: 9781501801747

Beautiful Already: Reclaiming God's Perspective on Beauty
Learning to see yourself as God sees you.

Workbook ISBN: 9781501813542

A Woman Overwhelmed: A Bible Study on the Life of Mary, the Mother of Jesus
Go from overwhelmed by life to overwhelmed by God.

Workbook ISBN: 9781501839924

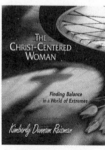

The Christ-Centered Woman: Finding Balance in a World of Extremes
Find balance and explore what the Bible teaches about Christ-centered living.

Workbook ISBN: 9781426773693

Anonymous: Discovering the Somebody You Are to God
Discover your significance to Christ by exploring some of the "anonymous" women of the Bible.

Workbook ISBN: 9781426792120

This I Know for Sure
Learn to live a life of unshakable faith and leave a spiritual legacy.

Workbook ISBN: 9781426772450

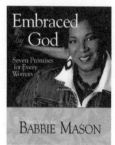

Embraced By God: Seven Promises for Every Woman
Explore the transformational power of God's love and acceptance.

Workbook ISBN: 9781426754418

A Woman's Place
Study a biblical look at vocation in the office, the home, in ministry, and beyond.

Participant Guide ISBN: 9781501849008

DVD, leader guide, and kit also available for each Bible study.
Find samples at AbingdonWomen.com